W0016730

STARTUP
GUIDE

#startupeverywhere

Startup Guide Warsaw

EDITORIAL
Publisher: Sissel Hansen
Editor: Marissa van Uden
Proofreaders: Emmanouil Fotakis,
Michelle Mills Smith

PRODUCTION
Global Production Lead: Eglė Duleckytė
Local Production Manager: Anastasia Ilcov
Research by Cláudia Letra

DESIGN & PHOTOGRAPHY
Designer: Daniela Castanheira
Illustrations by Cat Serafim, Daniela Castanheira,
Joana Carvalho
Photo Editors: Daniela Castanheira,
Joana Carvalho

PARTNERSHIPS
COO: Anna Weissensteiner
anna@startupguide.com

Printed by
Druckhaus Sportflug, Berlin
Sportflugstraße 5 -7, 12487 Berlin

Published by Startup Guide World ApS
Borgbjergsvej 1, 2450 Copenhagen

info@startupguide.com
startupguide.com

Worldwide distribution by Die Gestalten
gestalten.com

ISBN: 978-989-54894-6-6

WRITERS
Diana Figueroa (Packhelp P. 49, ProperGate P. 53,
Skriware P. 55, NEXT acceleration programme for female
founders P. 70-71, WARSAW booster P. 78-79, Kozminski
University P. 190-191, Inovo Venture Partners P. 202-203)
Don Clermont (SGH Warsaw School of Economics /
MBA for Startups P. 192-193)
Giovanna Centeno (LogicAI P. 47, Planet Heroes P. 51)
Hava Salsi (EcoBean P. 43, Akademickie Inkubatory
Przedsiębiorczości P. 60-61, foodtech.ac P. 62-63,
School of Pioneers P. 72-73, Brain Embassy P. 82-85,
WeWork P. 110-113,

Warsaw University of Technology Business School P. 196-197,
Next Road Ventures P. 206-207, PFR Ventures P. 208-209,
SMOK Ventures P. 210-211)
Kate Williams (City Profile by City of Warsaw P. 19-21,
Google for Startups P. 122-127, InnoEnergy P. 116-121, Santander
P. 128-133, Joanna Drabent P. 148-155, Jowita Michalska P.
156-163, Marcin Beme P. 164-171, Paweł Sieczkiewicz P. 172-179,
Vadym Melnyk P. 180-187)
Lucy Beckley (Authologic P. 41, Center of Entrepreneurship
Smolna (CES) P. 212-213, Foundation for Technology
Entrepreneurship P. 64-65, Microsoft for Startups P. 68-69,
ReaktorX P. 74-75, StartUp HUB Poland P. 76-77, CIC Warsaw
(Cambridge Innovation Center Warsaw) P. 90-93, Mindspace
Koszyki P. 106-109, University of Warsaw P. 194-195)
Rachel Velebny (Jutro Medical P. 45, HubHub P. 102-105,
AIP Seed P. 200-201)
Sarah Nagaty (Essentials P. 23-35, Apollo P. 39, Vue Storefront
P. 57, Google for Startups P. 66-67, Centrum Kreatywności
Targowa P. 86-89, District Hall P. 94-97,
Market One Capital P. 204-205)

LOCAL RESEARCH AND DATA
Ewa Geresz
The Polish Association of Centers for Technology
Transfer PACTT
Kazimierz Anhalt

PHOTOGRAPHER
Photography by Daniel Król P. 18-20, P. 42, P. 46, P. 48,
P. 52, P. 54, P. 66, P. 90-93, P. 94-97, P. 98-101, P. 122-125,
P. 128-131, P. 134-137, P. 140-143, P. 148-155, P. 156-163, P. 164-171,
P. 172-179, P. 180-187

ADDITIONAL PHOTOGRAPHY
Peter Bjerke P. 8 / Adam Tuchlinski P. 40 / Alicja Koczaska
P. 44 / Ryszard Waniek and Karolina Gurgul P. 50 /
Zosia Zija & Jacek Pioro P. 38 / Marcin Bracki P. 56 /
Sara Gugałka P. 60 / foodtech.ac P. 62 / Arvind Juneja
P. 64, Martyna Kędra P. 70 / Agata Kwasniewska P. 74 /
PFR communication department P. 72, P. 208 / Stanisław
Leszczyński P. 76 / Paweł Libera P. 78 / Brain Embassy
P. 82-85 / Polish Chamber of Commerce and Adrianna
Ojrzanowska P. 86-89 / Kataryna Nadrowska, Alicja Bokina
and Emilia Król P. 102-105 / Boaz Arad, Piotr Gromek and
Anny Gorajka P. 106-109 / Marian Chrzan, WeWork P. 110-113 /
Marzena Rej-Brodowska P. 116-119 / Szymon Krzyżanowski
P. 190 / Magdalena Meler P. 192 / Faculty of Management
University of Warsaw P. 194 / Monika Replin P. 196 / Inovo
Venture Partners P. 202 / Studio ART-D Dorota i Maciej
Fersten P. 204 / Next Road Ventures ASI Sp. z o.o. P. 206 /
Unsplash: Zhi Xuan Hew P. 6-7 / Victor Malyushev P. 22 /
Adam Borkowski P. 25 / Marcin Lukasik P. 26 / Bianca Fazacas
P. 28, P. 32 / Milana Jovanov P. 30 / Charlie Gallant P. 34 /
Economic Development Department of the City of Warsaw P. 212

Copyright © 2022 Startup Guide World ApS All rights reserved.

Although the authors and publisher have made every effort to ensure that the information in this book
was correct, they do not assume and hereby disclaim any liability to any party for any loss, damage,
or disruption caused by errors or omissions, whether such errors or omissions result from negligence,
accident, or any other cause. No part of this publication may be reproduced, distributed, or transmitted
in any form or by any means, including photocopying, recording, or other electronic or mechanical
methods, without the prior written permission of the publisher, except in the case of brief quotations
embodied in critical reviews and certain other non-commercial uses permitted by copyright law.

onetreeplanted.org

STARTUP GUIDE
WARSAW

STARTUP GUIDE WARSAW

In partnership with
Venture Café Warsaw Foundation

Proudly supported by

Google for Startups

**VENTURE
CAFÉ**
ᐯ
WARSAW

Sissel Hansen
/ Startup Guide

Well known for its rich history and being a leading economic hub, Warsaw is on a fast track to becoming the most startup-friendly city in Eastern Europe. The tech sector is especially highly developed here. The city is home to excellent technological institutes that ensure a large pool of talented software engineers and developers. The first-class STEM education and the relatively low cost of living also make Warsaw an increasingly attractive destination for many international students.

In recent years, Warsaw has experienced a tremendous increase in VC funding, with 2020 being a record year and almost half of invested capital coming from international funds. The establishment of the Polish Development Fund (PFR) in 2016 was a key driver in achieving this success. The organization is behind many financial and advisory institutions that work closely together to support innovation and entrepreneurship in the Polish capital.

There is also a healthy supply of many other local initiatives driving a new generation of entrepreneurs. The nonprofit foundation Startup Hub Poland is a key local player that offers multiple programs for startups as well as expert advice on scaling globally. Akademickie Inkubatory Przedsiębiorczości (AIP) is a program that provides a legal identity and all the necessary resources for starting a new business. Its sister organization, AIP Seed, is the investment fund with one of the largest portfolios in CEE.

Warsaw also offers excellent options when it comes to coworking spaces. Major international companies such as WeWork, Mindspace and Brain Embassy are located here, but there are also many local organizations that provide innovative environments for startups to work.

Through this book, we're thrilled to have had the opportunity to learn more about Warsaw and the people and organizations that drive its startup ecosystem. There is no doubt that the Polish capital has an exciting future ahead, and we'll definitely keep an eye on its further development. For now, we hope you will enjoy this overview of Warsaw's current entrepreneurial scene.

Rafał Trzaskowski
/ Mayor of Warsaw

Warsaw is a rapidly developing, open-minded metropolis. But its greatest asset is the people – educated, ambitious, driven and enterprising. It is they who build the innovative and creative potential of Poland's capital city.

Warsaw is the largest academic center in the country and one of the hot spots for R&D in the CEE region, drawing in people from other cities, regions and countries to pursue their dreams and professional ambitions. No wonder Warsaw is the heartland of Poland's startup business. An impressive one in three startups sets up shop in the capital city, creating the right ecosystem for innovation – an ecosystem made up of corporations, investment funds, the creative sector and business-support institutions.

Warsaw is a robust technology hub, as reflected in its strong performance in rankings of business- and technology-friendly cities. It is well poised to become a major location for startup support in CEE, and this is the goal we are going for. The city already plays a significant role in incubating startups from Eastern Europe, in particular Ukraine.

And, as a local government, we are committed to promoting entrepreneurship and creating the right conditions for new businesses to thrive. We operate municipal business centers in which entrepreneurs and those who plan to set up a company can take advantage of free-of-charge training, workshops, mentoring programs and individual counseling. For a couple of years now, we have had in place a free-of-charge municipal acceleration program to help creators and innovators hone their business competencies and develop their projects with the assistance of experts.

Our firm belief is that by supporting startup founders, we invest in Warsaw's development, as it is these kinds of people – driven, creative and innovative – that shape its future.

In Warsaw, people matter the most. We help them thrive and make their plans and dreams a reality.

Local Community Partner / Venture Café Warsaw Foundation

To understand Warsaw's potential you need to know its history. During World War II it was more than 90 percent destroyed and was reborn like a phoenix from the ashes, creating one of the most dynamically developing and modern innovation ecosystems in Europe.

The fast development took place only after 1989 with the fall of communism and the inflow of know-how and capital from outside, and the release of the entrepreneurial spirit. The "Iron Curtain" period caused a delay of about forty years in the country's development, but thanks to this, its boom came at a completely different time in terms of technological development, which allowed Warsaw to build modern infrastructure in many important sectors of the economy such as fintech, proptech and IoT.

Reconstruction of the city center with modern office buildings created opportunities unique in Europe to concentrate all key elements for the innovation ecosystem in one place. Top corporations choose Warsaw as the headquarters for their shared service centers because of its location, attractive cost of living and labor, rich human capital and high quality of life.

The beginning of building an innovation ecosystem started with the creation of entrepreneurship incubators at Warsaw universities in 2004. In 2007, Aula Polska, a cyclical meetup for the innovation industry, was established. In 2011, a small coworking space, Reaktor, began gathering a community around technology and innovation, and since 2015, the Startup Poland foundation has conducted an annual survey of the startup industry.

In 2015, the project of an organic innovation district in Warsaw kicked off, and Cambridge Innovation Center (CIC) and Venture Café Warsaw foundation became the leaders of this project. The opening of the CIC Innovation Campus in July 2020 coincided with the COVID-19 pandemic, but it soon became apparent that this is when infrastructure of this type is even more needed. Programs created by the foundation have become key points in sustaining relationships in the ecosystem.

We are glad that Warsaw will have its own *Startup Guide*, and that even more people in the world will be able to learn about the fantastic things happening in Poland.

Aureliusz Górski
Cofounder @ Cambridge Innovation Center in Poland
Founding Executive Director @ Venture Café Warsaw Foundation
Advisory Board Member @ Startup Poland

Ewa Geresz
Director of Programs and Partnerships @ Venture Café Warsaw Foundation

contents

STARTUP
GUIDE
WARSAW

startups

programs

spaces

experts

founders

schools

investors

Local Ecosystem

[Facts & Figures]
- Warsaw is Poland's largest academic center[1], with more than 70 tertiary institutions, over 200,000 students and 33 A+ public research establishments involved in research and development.[2]
- 30% of foreign students in Poland pursue higher education in Warsaw.[3]
- There are about 40,000 foreign citizens living in Warsaw.[4]
- Warsaw is a major business location and a leader in Central and Eastern Europe (CEE) in terms of economic development and office-market maturity.[5]
- There are more than 50 VC funds and over 40 business-support institutions in Warsaw, making it the top business location in Poland.[6]
- Warsaw is the number-one place for investment, according to the "Warsaw's Investment Potential" report.[7]
- In the fDi European Cities and Regions of the Future 2020/21 ranking, Warsaw came second in the category of business-friendly cities.

[Notable Startups]
- Covid Genomics, a machine-learning startup specializing in enhancing mRNA vaccines and drug discovery, raised €970,000.[8]
- ExploRNA Therapeutics develops breakthrough mRNA modification technologies that open the way to anti-cancer applications and vaccinations. The company's CEO, Prof. Jacek Jemielity from University of Warsaw, received the 2021 Foundation for Polish Science (FNP) Prize in chemistry and materials sciences for developing chemical modifications of mRNA as tools for therapeutic applications and studies on cellular processes.[9]
- Science 4 Beauty, a high-research startup developing a new generation of anti-wrinkle solutions powered by a neurotoxins family that can be used also in drug development, raised almost €1 million.[10]

[1]Warsaw Statistical Yearbook 2020, link: Urząd Statystyczny w Warszawie / Publikacje i foldery / Roczniki Statystyczne; [2]Report: "Warsaw – A Space for Research and Development", the Warsaw University of Technology, the Centre for Innovation and Technology Transfer Management of the Warsaw University of Technology (CZIiTT PW), 2019; [3]The Academicness of Polish cities, the Polish Economic Institute, Warsaw 2019, link: PIE-Raport_Akademickość.indd; "Diagnosis for the "We Attract Talents and Leaders" implementation program as part of the "#Warsaw2030 Strategy", 2019; [5]Warsaw Your Place, Warsaw 2021, link: Warsaw Your Place - Warszawa Twoje Miejsce - Biznes (um.warszawa.pl); [6]Diagnosis for the "We Drive Innovation" implementation program as part of the "#Warsaw2030 Strategy", 2019, link: Program generujemy innowacje - Strategia (um.warszawa.pl); [7]"Warsaw's Investment Potential" report, 1st edition, Antal Study, Warsaw 2018; [8]covidgenomics.com; [9]fnp.org.pl/en/prof-jacek-jemielity-laureat-nagrody-fnp-2021; [10]gov.pl/attachment/6b5c078e-1036-4211-bd76-9093a79087f3 (Rekomendowana kwota dofinansowania); [11]Statistics Poland, Dec. 2020; [12]rcin.org.pl/Content/157600/WA51_188627_r2020-t92-z4_Przeg-Geogr-Sleszyns.pdf; [13]warszawa.stat.gov.pl/download/gfx/warszawa; [14]Statistics Poland, June 2021

[City] # Warsaw, Poland

[Statistics]

Population[11]: 1,794,166
Population projections[12]: 2030: 2,132,000; 2050: 2,249,000
Area: 517.2 km²
GDP per capita[13]: 163,372 zł (2018)
Rate of unemployment[14]: 2%

STARTUP GUIDE WARSAW

Global Vision, Local Focus – How Warsaw Is Working toward Startup Success

Karolina Zdrodowska / Head Coordinator for Entrepreneurship and Social Dialogue, City of Warsaw

Maciej Sadowski / CEO, Startup Hub Poland Foundation

Warsaw has big plans for the future. Already a major political, economic and cultural center, Poland's capital city has now set its sights on becoming a startup hub. "We've set ourselves the goal of becoming a center for entrepreneurship in Eastern Europe by 2040," says Karolina Zdrodowska. "Many of the activities in our 2030 Warsaw Strategy roadmap are working towards this."

Located at the heart of Central and Eastern Europe and home to big-name multinationals such as Google and Oracle, the city is already a great place to start a business. Entrepreneurs benefit from good transport and ecosystem connections to hubs like Berlin and Prague and to talent markets like Central and Eastern Europe, and in particular Ukraine. The city also boasts excellent educational institutions but without the exorbitant salaries, rents and cost of living of other major European cities, which helps startup funding go further. And while homegrown investment funds are a relatively recent development, Poland is making up for lost time with a mushrooming VC community.

"We have a great academic offer that draws innovative, talented people," says Karolina. "We aim to get them to stay after graduation, and we think they'll be glad they did. When we measure satisfaction levels among Warsaw ecosystem members, eighty-two percent say they wouldn't live anywhere else."

A steady supply of top STEAM talent has also contributed to boosting the city's standing as a regional leader in biotech, ICT, cybersecurity, cloud computing, data science and machine learning. But it's not resting on its laurels. "There are five sectors where we want to become leaders," says Karolina. "We're already strong in business services and green municipal economy, and we're working to add creative, agri-food and bioeconomy to the list."

In line with these aims, the City has been working hard in recent decades to create a startup-friendly environment where entrepreneurs can access support and networking and find collaborators, talent and investment. To date, it's produced names like DocPlanner, Allegro and CD Projekt Red as well as leading scientists involved in collaborations with NASA and the European Space Agency.
"Our benchmarks in terms of innovation hubs are Tel Aviv and Stockholm," says Maciej Sadowski. "That's what we're aiming for."

To achieve its goals, the City has established a multidisciplinary working group featuring representatives from local government, accelerators, incubators, coworking spaces and associations to share information and promote initiatives that support entrepreneurs. It also organizes events such as the Warsaw Startup Nights to bring entrepreneurs together with international businesses. The Warsaw Booster accelerator and regular Technology Reviews also serve to strengthen ecosystem cooperation and connect startups to potential customers by connecting them to representatives from established companies and municipal departments. "Cooperation between the private sector, the third sector and the City is really good here," says Maciej. "We get a lot of support, we have a fully open and very honest dialogue, and full access to Karolina and her team."

In terms of physical spaces, there's the Zodiac Business Pavilion, an economic showroom for Warsaw businesses; and the Smolna Center for Entrepreneurship, a one-stop advisory for entrepreneurs that helps with everything from registering a company to accessing local institutions and training. In line with the City's creative sector ambitions, the Targowa 56 Center of Creativity offers affordable rental space and free lectures, workshops and training. It's open both to companies and residents of the local underprivileged neighborhood. The aim is to foster connections with the local community and ensure business activities focus on local issues and benefit the local economy. "We want to create a network of local connections," says Karolina, "so entrepreneurs feel they are working in a local environment and can not only rely on the help of the City but also develop their business locally."

Looking further afield, Warsaw collaborates closely with the City of Dusseldorf and the Vienna Business Agency, and the city's companies and business institutions are regular participants at initiatives like the Digital Demo Day tech fair and Startup Woche Dusseldorf.

"There's so much going on here now," says Maciej. "A few years ago when I was in California, people told me, 'Maciej, Europe ends at Berlin. There's nothing east of Berlin.' And now I see them coming here, so it looks like their maps have expanded a bit."

About

The City of Warsaw promotes innovation and entrepreneurship through favorable economic policy, home-grown initiatives and events, collaborations with other regional business hubs, and projects involving public, private and third-sector partners.

Established in 2012, Startup Hub Poland is a nonprofit foundation that promotes the growth of high-tech startups in Central and Eastern Europe. Its mission is to connect disruptive technologies and business models with financing and expertise and offer practical advice, for example, related to company registration, work permits and corporate relationships.

[Contact]   Email: kontakt@um.warszawa.pl

[Links]   Web: um.warszawa.pl LinkedIn: company/grow-with-warsaw
Facebook: CentrumPrzedsiebiorczosciSmolna Twitter: @warszawa

Cityscape, Warsaw

Intro to the City

Warsaw is the capital and largest city of Poland, the biggest economy in Central and Eastern Europe (CEE). With a metropolitan area home to over three million people, it boasts a thriving cultural scene and one of the highest proportions of green space of any urban area in Europe. The city's rebuilt old town is a UNESCO World Heritage Site featuring virtually every era of European architectural history. Warsaw, strategically placed at the midpoint between London, Moscow, Stockholm and Budapest, has also been at the forefront of Poland's growth this century in sectors such as IT, business services and gamedev. As Poland's economy has advanced dramatically with the highest growth rate across the continent since 1990, Warsaw has a high potential to become a deeptech hub.

Google and Microsoft are just two of the industry leaders to have set up their own hubs in Warsaw for work in areas ranging from cloud solutions to biotech. This advance in the deeptech industry has followed the development of higher education in Poland. Warsaw University of Technology is one of the leading tech institutes in Europe, while the University of Warsaw ranks in the top few CEE universities. As a result, Polish software developers are rated the third best in the world. Warsaw is also among the top ten financial centers in CEE, and the number of cargo shipments its Warsaw Chopin Airport processes is rising 15 percent annually. Prior to the COVID pandemic, the city attracted ten million tourists in the average year.

Before You Come

Although summers in Warsaw are generally warm, it is known for subzero temperatures in winter. You'll need to pack something for each season and include snowproof clothing. House-hunting is challenging, so searching online before arriving can help. Be prepared to stay at a hotel, a short-term rental or with a friend while searching. Once you are a resident in Warsaw, you must register your address with the local authority, which requires a tenancy agreement and proof of your right to reside in Poland or another Schengen-Area country. Driving licenses for any EU or EEA country are valid to use in Poland. If your driver's licence is not from EU/EFTA, it is valid for six months in Poland from the day you register yourself in Warsaw. After this, you are required to pass a driving-theory test to exchange it for a valid Polish licence.

Visas and Work Permits

Poland is a part of the European Union's Schengen Area, meaning any EU-national is free to live, work and start a business there, as are third-country nationals with permanent residence, long-term EU residence, a spousal visa, or student or research residence. For other third-country nationals, fully licensed and incorporated employers must sponsor and secure a visa and work permit for prospective employees. They must conduct a labor-market test to prove there is no eligible Polish or EU national who could be employed instead. This test is not needed if the local *Voivode* (official) has included the particular field of work in a list of high-demand jobs. Work permits have a duration of three years, but, depending on the type, work visas may last only six months or one year. The entire visa application process generally takes three to four weeks for approval, but may extend to up to eight weeks.

You can obtain permanent residence (and eligibility for citizenship after five years) by investing a minimum of €100,000 ($118,300) in a form of Polish commercial activity. You can also secure a temporary residence permit by setting up a startup that is able to generate €15,000 ($17,700) a year. After three years of temporary residence on this basis, you will qualify for permanent residence. Investment in real estate qualifies as a form of commercial activity in both of these cases.

See **Important Government Offices** page **216**

Palace of Culture and Science, Warsaw

Red bicycle on a street, Warsaw

Cultural Differences

Warsaw fuses traditional elements of Polish culture with the conveniences of a modern European capital. You can sample the staple Polish delicacies such as *pierogi* (crescent-shaped dumplings) *gołąbki* (stuffed cabbage leaves) and *kanapki* (open sandwiches) at any local restaurant or *bar mleczny (milk bar)*. Warsaw is becoming a vegan-friendly city offering vegan food prepared from local products. Breakfast is popular and can be served up until 2:00 PM. In warm weather, open-air breakfast markets are held on weekends. *Obiad* (lunch) is usually taken after 2:00 PM. Polish mead is experiencing a revival in popularity, as many Warsaw pubs and microbreweries will attest to. Festivals run throughout the year, from the traditional Procession of the Three Kings in January to the Festival of Contemporary Music in the fall and open Chopin concerts in a historic park. Polish people value generosity, courtesy and the reciprocation of these values. They tend to build personal relationships when doing business. As when moving to any country, it is important to maintain respect and familiarize yourself with the country's history before starting any conversations about more sensitive topics.

Cost of Living

At the time of writing, the Polish złoty (zł) exchanged at an average of 3.82 zł to the US dollar and 4.55 zł to the euro. The Mapping the World's Prices 2019 report by Deutsche Bank lists Warsaw as having the twelfth lowest cost of living. A single person's average monthly expenses without rent are approximately 2,823 zł ($740), and the average monthly salary is 4,580 zł ($1,199). A two-room apartment of 50 m^2 located in central Warsaw costs 2,500 zł ($617) to 3200 zł ($838) per month to rent. Household bills could come to 1,000 zł ($260), while public transport passes are 110 zł ($26). On average, a 500 ml glass of local beer costs 12 zł ($3) and a two-course meal including soup comes to 30 zł ($8). Poland's government-funded, insurance-based health system affords large parts of society, including employees and their families, free healthcare. This applies to all residents, including those with temporary permits. However, private health insurance is commonly provided to foreign employees by their companies.

Mermaid of Warsaw, Warsaw

Accommodation

The website **rentflatpoland.com** is specifically designed for house-hunting in Poland as an expat. The housing sections of **gratka.pl** and **olx.pl** also have listings updated daily. There are groups on Facebook also dedicated to searching for accommodation in Warsaw. It is acceptable to take a room in shared accommodation if necessary. There are two types of rental agreements with landlords allowed in Poland: private (informal) agreements akin to subletting and formal tenancy agreements. Informal agreements are common but can cause paperwork issues for the tenant; for example, when they try to open a bank account. Tenancy agreements typically have a duration of six or twelve months. Guarantors are usually not required, but there could be a deposit payment of two or even three months' rent up front. Household bills tend to be excluded from the agreement.

See **Accommodation** page **215**

Insurance

Social Insurance is compulsory for anyone who works in Poland, payable in part by employers and in part by employees. This insurance breaks down into several categories, the main ones being pension insurance (split equally between the employer and employee), disability pension insurance (covered largely by the employer), health insurance, and accident and illness insurance (covered by the employee). The Polish Investment and Trade Agency (PAIH) gives a full breakdown of Social Insurance payment rates (**paih.gov.pl/polish_law/taxation/pit**). Those who are self-employed usually cover the whole cost of both parts of their insurance, but if you are on a *umowa zlecenie* (commission contract) the Polish Social Insurance Institution (ZUS) covers your retirement, disability and health insurance.

See **Insurance Companies** page **217**

Roman Catholic Church of the Visitants, Warsaw

Starting a Company

The conditions for registering a company in Warsaw depend on whether you are starting a capital company, a partnership or a sole proprietorship. For a sole proprietorship, extra restrictions apply for citizens who are not from the EU, UK, US or Switzerland. No startup capital is needed to register a partnership, but a limited liability capital company requires 5,000 zł ($1,309) in investment, and a joint-stock capital company would need to raise 50,000 zł ($12,350). Although you don't need to be a resident to start a company in Poland, it must have a Poland-based director and you would need a business visa to travel to Poland to work there. Even then, the success of the application is not guaranteed. Hiring at least two Polish employees in your company would increase your chances.

When registering your company, you can consult the Polish government's business website for help (**biznes.gov.pl/en/firma/doing-business-in-poland/company-registration-in-poland**). For direct advice, they also have a virtual assistant and phone number accessible (**biznes.gov.pl/pl/centrum-pomoc**). You may need a fluent Polish-speaker to translate for you, which is also advisable for the registration process itself. If registering a sole proprietorship and using your home address in Warsaw, you should inform your landlord, as they may be charged extra property taxes. The fee varies, and the process is carried out by district courts, taking around two weeks.

See **Programs** page **58**

Opening a Bank Account

You need only a residence permit and a passport to open a bank account in Poland. Certain banks that market to foreigners, such as Santander Bank Polska, ING Bank Śląski and Millennium Bank may need only your passport and proof of residence in your country of origin. The four biggest banks in Poland (PKO BP and the three mentioned above) offer both business and personal banking. You can transfer up to €10,000 ($11,500) to or from accounts in Poland without any declaration. ATMs (*Bankomat*) are widely available in Warsaw, though in more rural areas it is advisable to bring cash. Machines charge fees for foreign credit and debit cards. In most cases, you need a bank account in Poland to start a business there, unless it is a micro-company with few employees and a low turnover. For sole proprietorships, it is possible to run the business through your personal bank account with lower fees, although this may cause complications with paperwork.

See **Banks** page **215**

ROKU 1861.

Detail of building in Krakowskie Przedmieście street, W...

Taxes

The standard corporation tax rate in Poland is 19 percent. There is no separate capital gains tax. Companies with revenues below €2 million ($2.2million) may apply for a lower corporation tax rate of 9 percent. See the Polish government's business website: **biznes.gov.pl/en/firma.** An additional minimum business income tax, deductible from standard corporation tax, was introduced in 2022 to target tax avoidance. It is levied on corporations reporting minimal profits or losses, at a rate equivalent to 10 percent of their tax base. The standard VAT rate is 23 percent but there are reduced rates of 8 percent and 5 percent on gas, electricity, particular foods, media and services. Income taxation in Poland is progressive with two brackets. The upper bracket pays 15,300 zł ($4,000) plus 32 percent on the excess over 120,000 zł ($31,400). Income tax is paid by all residents and non-residents employed in Poland. Personal income tax declarations are submitted annually between February and April 30. Companies in Warsaw are subject to research and development tax breaks, and new low-income enterprises have an exemption on 30 percent of their corporation tax for the six years after the launch of their product (see **biznes.gov.pl/pl/portal/001099**).

See **Financial Services** page **216**

Phone and Internet

Prices for monthly mobile phone plans in Poland range from 5 zł ($1.30) to 71 zł ($19). Popular providers are T-Mobile, Orange Polska, Play and Plus. Contract lengths tend to be one year. Home internet plans are usually two years. Netia is the exception with a nine-month contract offer, and Play offers a pay-as-you-go option. The main option for business internet is DSL TP from Orange Polska. Orange Polska also provides one of the two main plans for home internet, along with Netia's Net24. Download speeds tend to vary between 10 Mbit/s and 80 Mbit/s. The average internet bill for 60 Mbit/s or more with unlimited data is 71 zł ($19).

Getting Around

Warsaw is the intersection for major road, rail and air routes across Central and Eastern Europe. Warsaw Chopin Airport is 10 km from the city center and easily reachable by train, bus or taxi, and Warszawa Modlin Airport serves several budget airlines. Express trains run daily to and from Berlin, Vilnius, Kiev and Moscow, among other cities, with discount prices when booked in advance. Kraków is two and half hours south on the InterCity railway, and Gdansk is three and half hours north. Within Warsaw, two metro lines, a tram and a day-night bus system are all fast and efficient ways to get around. The city's roads are usually congested, but Warsaw's electric scooter and public bike-sharing systems offer an alternative. You get a free twenty-minute ride each time you rent a bike from one of the three hundred stations around the city. There are over 680 km (422 miles) of cycle paths to explore. Uber and Bolt are also readily available at low prices.

Łazienki Park, Warsaw

Learning the Language

The EF English Proficiency Index (2021) ranks Warsaw as the fourteenth city in the "Very High Proficiency" band globally. Although you can get by without learning the language, doing so will be a big plus when starting a business, especially in handling administrative tasks with local authorities. Any effort you put into speaking Polish will be greatly appreciated by locals, and older Poles tend not to speak English. Polish may seem intimidating when you see it written down, as there are so many accents and pronunciation doesn't always follow spelling. It does use the Roman alphabet, though, unlike other Slavic languages, and immersion is the key to getting used to the sounds. Polish language courses in Warsaw range from individual tutors to group classes and intensive, slower-paced programs, and a standard one-hour class can cost around 60 zł ($16), for example at the British Council language school (**britishcouncil.pl/en**).

See **Language Schools** page **217**

Meeting People

Pub crawls are customary for giving newcomers to Warsaw the chance to get to know the city and meet new people. There are many organizing groups on Facebook and TripAdvisor, and a website dedicated to the custom (**pubcrawl.pl**). Meetup offers several Warsaw-based English language groups, including one for expats and another for language exchange, and a Discussion and Inspiration group for Digital Society and Culture. The Professional Women's Network has an active chapter in Warsaw, and there is the Warsaw Network: a forum of think tanks linked to the Warsaw Enterprise Institute which holds its own events. You can rent a place at dozens of coworking spaces dotted around the city, including several Regus locations, for as little as 25 zł ($6.50) a day. Most of the startup events in Poland take place in Warsaw, such as Pixel Heaven, Women in Tech Summit or Venture Café Thursday Gatherings, attracting many tech specialists and entrepreneurs, while Venture Café Warsaw's District Hall at the city's Cambridge Innovation Center (**cic.com/en/warsaw**) describes itself as the "first public innovation center in the world."

ups

[Name]

Apollo

[Elevator Pitch]

"We produce plant-based chicken made of white beans with a technology used nowhere else in the world."

[The Story]

The idea for Apollo (formerly Roślinny Qurczak) came to CEO Iga Czubak when she decided to stop eating meat. Since meat is a crucial part of Polish cuisine, Iga had to find an alternative. She experimented with a new technology that allows for producing plant-based chicken made of white beans, and the result was a product that has all the amino acids found in meat as well as a very similar texture to meat. What started out as a dietary adaptation to personal needs became an idea for a potential business. Iga joined an acceleration program, which helped her turn her new plant-based meat technology into a product for the market. An environmental and ethical motivation stands behind the product, which caters to not only the needs of vegetarians and vegans but also to those who would like to reduce their meat intake.

The company began cooking for big events and then started supplying restaurants. When the pandemic started, Apollo had to adapt to the market's needs and went online. The company managed to sell out in twenty-four hours of going online and had to produce faster to keep up with the market's demand. The product is now making its way to major supermarket chains in Poland.

[Funding History]

Bootstrap   Angel   External

Apollo started with personal funds. The first investment round involved business angels and raised €250,000 ($299,600). This allowed for an eighty-fold increase in production capacity. The next investment round will involve venture capital.

[Milestones]

- Changing the business model to adapt to the pandemic.

- Building our own infrastructure and equipment needed for bigger production plans.

- Closing our first investment round.

- Having our product feature soon in Carrefour and other major chain supermarkets.

- Launching a new, international brand Apollo.

[Links]   Web: apollo.store LinkedIn: company/eatapollo Facebook: eatapollo
Instagram: @eatapollo

Orchestration and Aggregation Layer for
local eKYC methods
supporting Antifraud Behavioural Scoring
Chargeback Fraud Prevention
Global Customer Onboarding
Compliance & High Conversion Rates
MacBook Pro

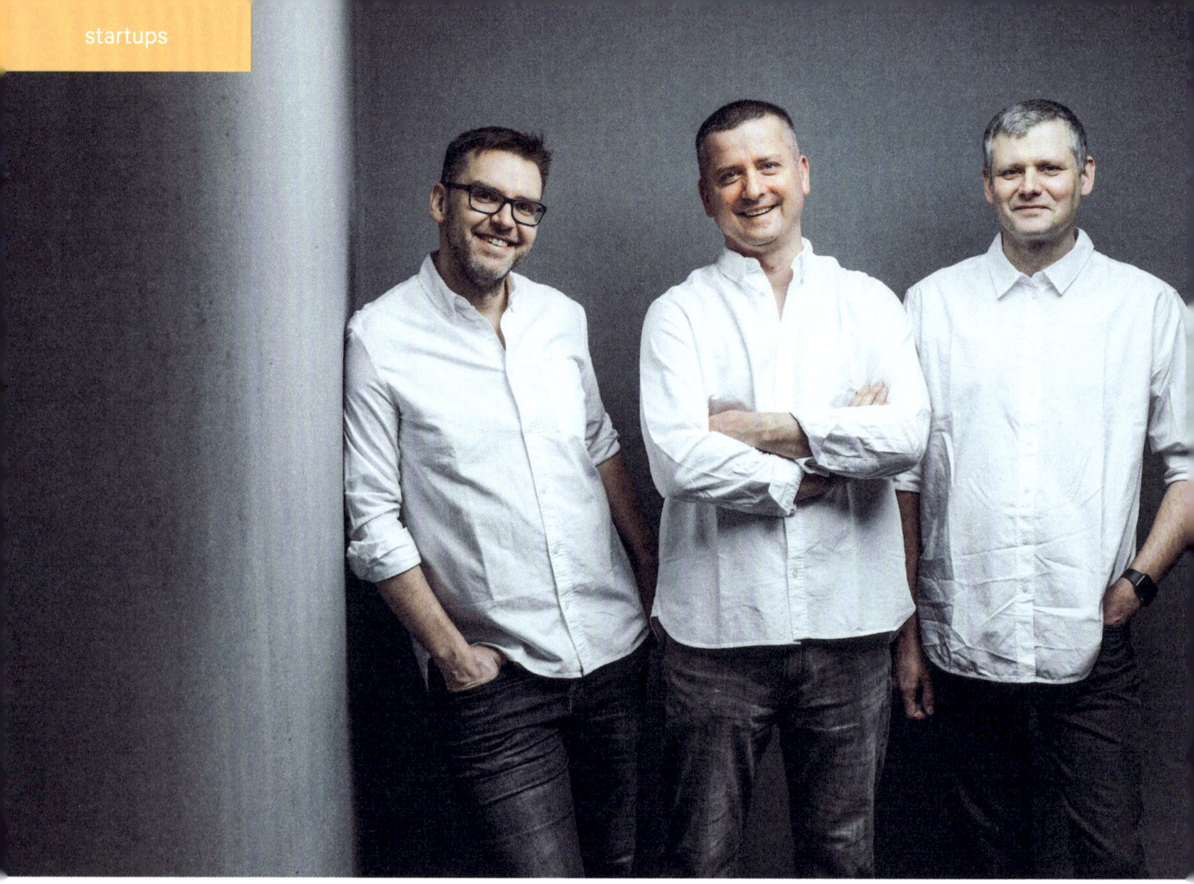

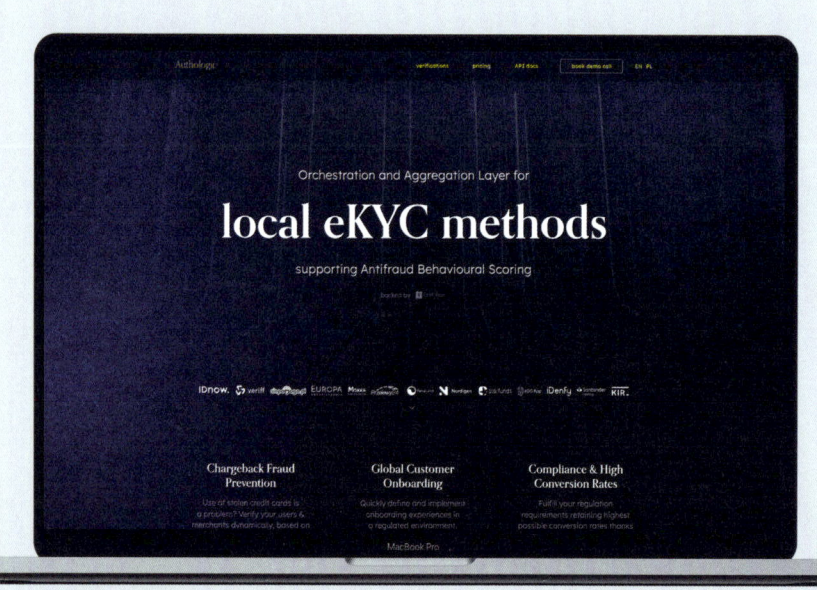

Authologic

[Elevator Pitch]

"We create an identity layer for the internet. We simplify ID verification by aggregating multiple methods into a single API. With Authologic, you can build advanced KYC processes faster, making it easier to identify your users."

[The Story]

Krzysztof Klimczak, Marek Rogoziński and Jarek Sygitowicz were cofounders of a company called ZenCard, which they successfully sold to the largest central bank in Europe in 2017. While working on a new credit product for the bank, they encountered problems with the online identification verification. The whole process was manual and clunky: users had to take a photograph of their document and then a selfie, and then additional steps were often required by the verifier. There was no quick and easy way to do it. In 2020, they decided to leave the bank to explore how they could fix this.

Through their research, they discovered that the reality of building a single method of online verification was unfeasible, so they set about combining the three main ID verification methods (document scanning, government-issued digital IDs and banks as identity verifiers) into one API. In July 2020, they launched Authologic. "We wanted to make it easier and faster for people to verify their identity online," says Jarek, "and instead of replacing the current identification methods, we decided to aggregate the methods into one API. Our ultimate aim is to build an identity layer for the internet, to simplify the process for both users and businesses. We see ourselves as Stripe for identity verification."

[Funding History]

Bootstrap   Angel   Pre-Seed

Seed   External

Initially, the founders bootstrapped. By October 2020, they closed a round of pre-seed investment, and in December 2020, within four weeks of completing the Y Combinator program, they raised seed funding. So far, they have raised over $2 million and are on track to raise their planned Series A funding in 2022.

[Milestones]

- Incorporating the company in July 2020 and rapidly gaining interest from potential customers.

- Closing a round of pre-seed investment by October 2020.

- Taking part in Y Combinator and raising funding within four weeks of finishing the program.

- Launching our new product in February 2021 and raising over $2 million.

[Links]   Web: **authologic.com** LinkedIn: **company/authologic** Twitter: **@authologic**

[Name] # EcoBean

[Elevator Pitch] *"We turn coffee waste into valuable raw materials and green products, decreasing the carbon footprint in the entire value chain within the coffee industry."*

[The Story] Coffee plays a major role in the lives of many worldwide. However, with extremely high demand comes an extremely large amount of waste that ultimately ends up in landfills, generating high carbon and methane emissions. The desire to reduce this waste drove cofounders Marcin Koziorowski and Kacper Kossowski to create EcoBean in 2018. "Here in Warsaw, we produce more than thirty to forty tons of coffee waste every day," says Marcin. Kacper, who had twenty years of experience in the coffee industry, initially approached Marcin with the idea to create coffee briquettes. However, noticing that making fires was not a big trend in Poland due to several environmental factors, they "started thinking in different ways," says Marcin.

EcoBean repurposes coffee waste collected from cafes, offices and gas stations to create raw materials such as coffee oil, coffee lignin, lactic acid and animal feed additives. These materials are used to produce a range of bioproducts such as straws, flowerpots and utensils, as well as coffee briquettes. Since its founding, the startup has expanded its network to include more partners to provide the needed coffee waste, which translates into more bioproducts. EcoBean's current project is to build the world's first biorefinery for coffee-waste valorization. The first three biorefineries will operate in Warsaw, Lisbon and Berlin with plans to expand in the future.

[Funding History]

Pre-Seed   Seed   External

EcoBean started with a pre-seed investment from KIC InnoEnergy, a venture capital firm funded by the European Union, who has now also committed to €1.4 million ($1.7 million) in the seed round. Currently, EcoBean is looking for a coinvestor in order to progress with its mission.

[Milestones]

- Setting up our research and development center at Warsaw University of Technology.
- Finding our first investor.
- Establishing our proof of concept with market leaders.
- Developing the technologies needed to create biorefineries.

[Links] Web: ecobean.pl LinkedIn: company/eco-bean Facebook: ecobeanPL
Twitter: @EcoBean_pl

[Name] # Jutro Medical

[Elevator Pitch] *"We are a new type of medical clinic where doctors can provide more comprehensive and preventative care. Our technology platform saves time, enabling doctors to address issues before they arise and extending and improving patients' quality of life."*

[The Story] In 2018, Adam Janczewski went to a routine optometrist appointment where, thanks to cancellations, his doctor had more time to spend with him and caught a serious genetic condition before it could do irreparable damage. While recovering, Adam realized he could build a new kind of clinic, where technology could help turn his experience into the basic standard of care. After two years of research, he founded Jutro Medical, which combines telemedicine and a proprietary technology platform with physical public clinics. Patient intake is done over the phone or online, and the software provides clinic staff a clear "dashboard" overview of patient information, giving doctors more time to spend on preventative care.

As CEO, Adam faced a considerable challenge in opening public clinics and finding early investors. In Poland's government-administered health service, the clinics needed approval, and profits depend solely on the number of patients. "When talking with investors, I was simply honest: we have a huge risk in national health insurance, but we don't have a lot of risks in patient acquisition or technology," says Adam. With an initial investor, Jutro Medical launched in January 2020. By July, the company had received a contract from the national health service. Although its planned clinic processes were disrupted by the pandemic, the team adapted to the challenge, growing from fourteen to eighty employees within a year, with monthly patient growth over 20 percent and 96 percent of consultations rated four out of five or higher.

[Funding History]

Angel   Pre-Seed   Seed

Jutro Medical's initial business angel invested €500,000 ($583,000). In September 2020, it received €1 million ($1.6 million) in pre-seed funding from eight investors, and in July 2021 it received €6 million ($7.6 million) from four investors, led by Inovo Venture Partners.

[Milestones]

- Launching the company in January 2020.
- Opening the first clinic in May 2020.
- Getting a contract with the national health insurance system in July 2020.
- Receiving €6 million in seed investment in July 2021.

[Links] Web: jutromedical.com/en LinkedIn: company/jutromedical Facebook: jutromedical
Instagram: @jutromedical Twitter: @JutroMedical

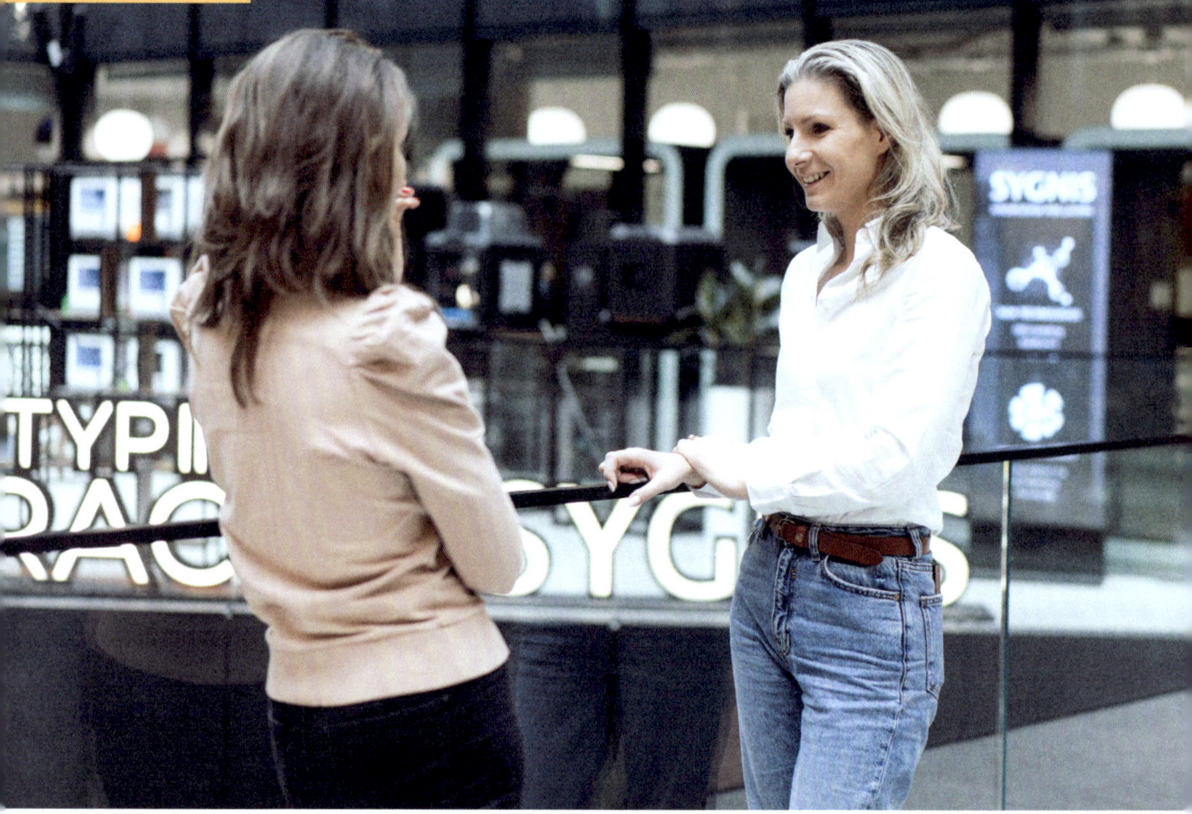
SYGNIS

Get happy and loyal customers

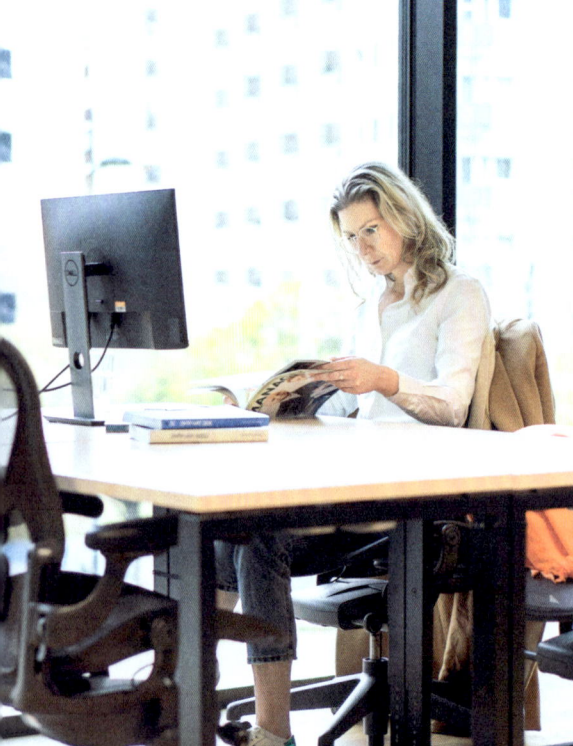

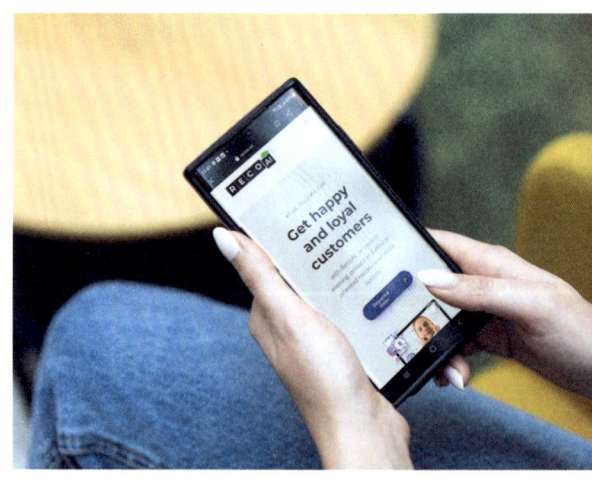

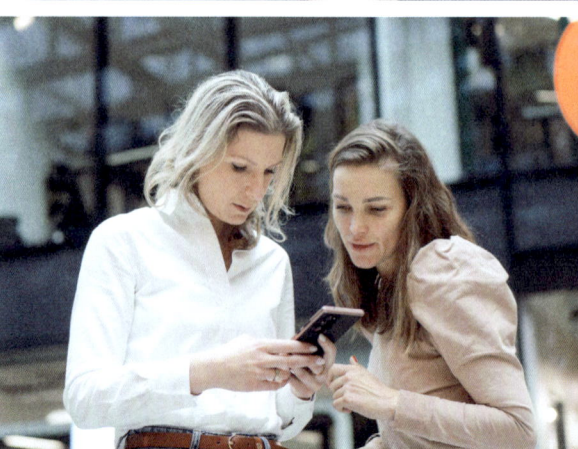

[Name] # LogicAI

[Elevator Pitch] *"We create tailored AI solutions for each client's individual needs, with top industry professionals and the latest technology. We provide you with greater knowledge of your customer base, so your business can thrive on smarter and faster solutions."*

[The Story] Maria Parysz and Paweł Jankiewicz, the founders of LogicAI, had previously worked in different tech companies in Warsaw, but they realized that the field of technology learning and AI was not growing fast enough in their home country of Poland. "Twenty years ago, nobody in Warsaw even knew what a data scientist was," says Maria. The two decided to go independent and start their own company. Now LogicAI is one of the top contenders in the field of data development. It works with companies such as Rolls Royce and LVMH to develop better data-gathering software that not only helps their customers' experience but also uses privacy-driven ethics to guarantee customer privacy.

More recently, LogicAI has started expanding into data security, working with the Dubai Police to create better cybersecurity strategies. "People are the future," says Maria. "We want to continue to expand our community of professionals and invest in them." LogicAI already has one of the most significant data-scientist communities in the world, with around seven million international participants. As the company looks to the future, its horizons are expanding westward; it is currently in the process of opening offices in Canada and its next big step is the North American market. The founders hope this move will expand their outreach and the image of Warsaw as a new nest for tech talent.

[Funding History]

Bootstrap

LogicAI was started with the private investments of its two founders and continues to be a bootstrap operation. It has not received any outside investment since founding, and as its client base has grown, it has become entirely self-reliant as a company.

[Milestones]

- Opening the Dubai office in 2019 and the Canada office in 2021.
- Winning the Recsys Challenge in 2019, the most prominent competition for recommendation systems.
- Reaching seven million data scientists in the Kaggle Days data-science community.
- RecoAI, our latest software, winning several global startup awards and competitions such as EU Tech Chamber, OVH Global startup, Latam Startup and HerStory Canada in 2021.

[Links] Web: **logicai.io** LinkedIn: **company/logicai** Facebook: **LogicAIofficial**

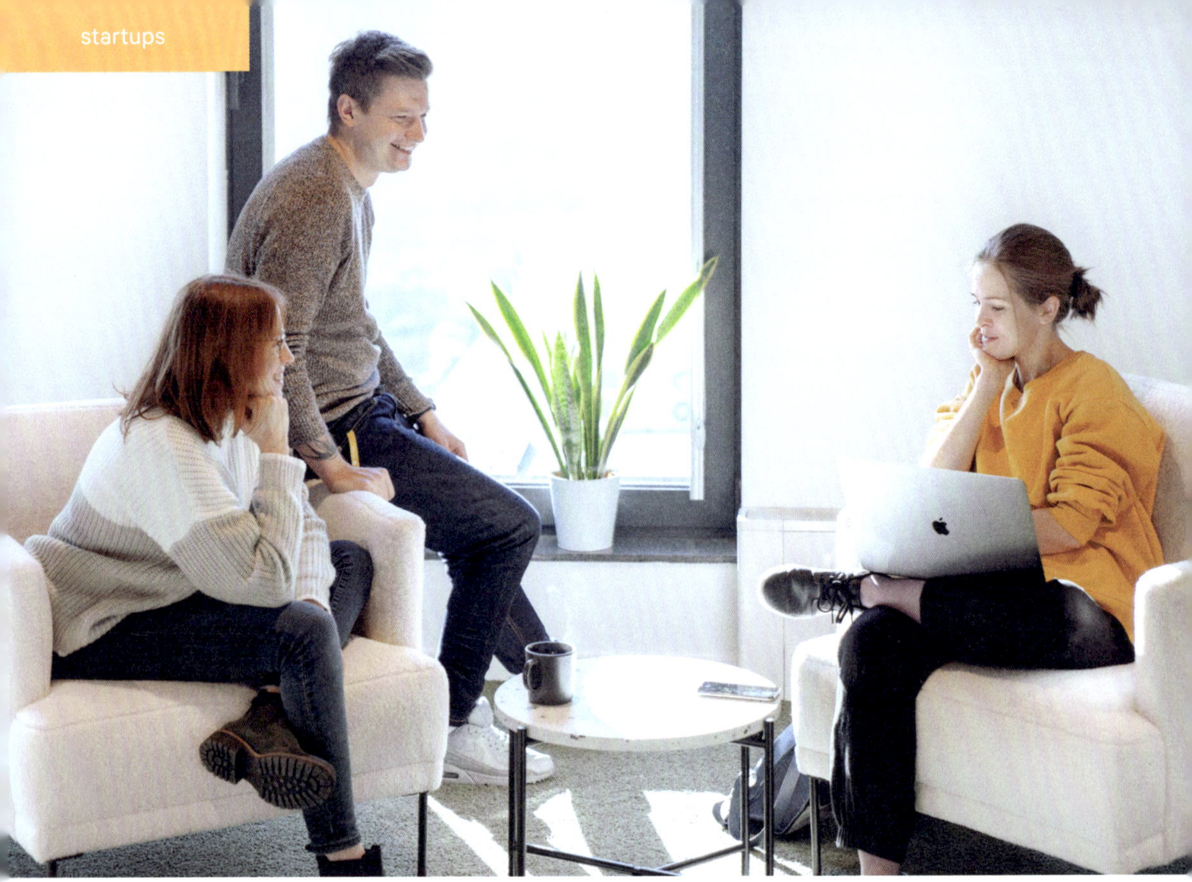

Show me
what you got!
Looking good

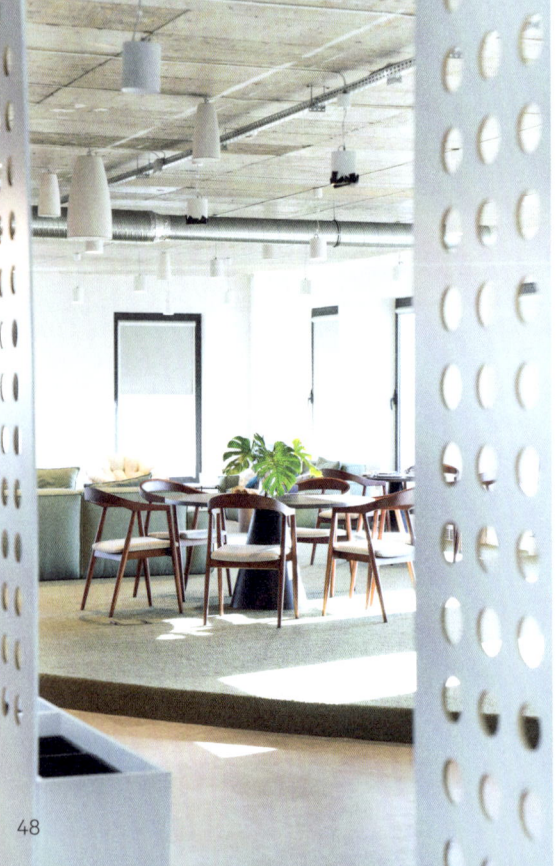

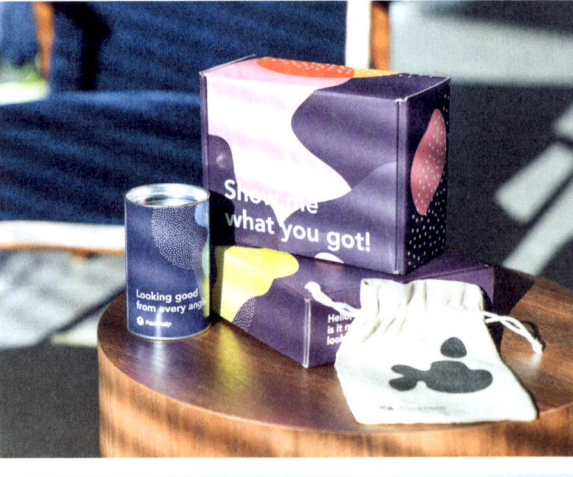

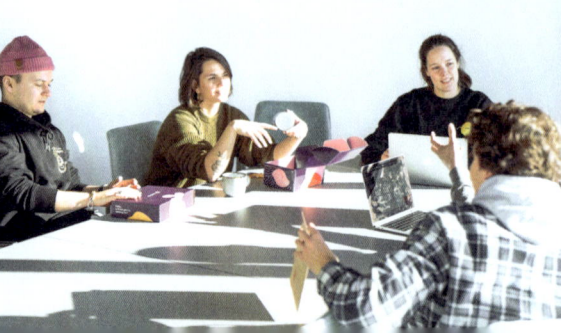

[Name] # Packhelp

[Elevator Pitch] *"We are an online marketplace for custom-branded packaging that provides innovative solutions for ecommerce brands, retailers, agencies and enterprises."*

[The Story] Packhelp helps brands to be better at packaging. Its intuitive web app allows customers to design, customize and order their own packaging in just a few clicks. Its proprietary software speeds up packaging development and automates mundane tasks, allowing companies to redirect their attention to other parts of their business that might need more attention. Packhelp's aim is to become the leading custom-packaging platform in the world by empowering brands to be better and more creative with their packaging ideas and services, and its top priority in achieving this is to help brands transition to custom-branded packaging solutions that are 100 percent sustainable.

Its vast network of suppliers enables it to be a single partner for all types of customer packaging needs, producing products from envelopes and bags to food packaging and typographic boxes. Since its founding in 2017, the company has optimized the company to work on larger, more complex packaging projects and has enabled over fifty thousand customers in more than thirty countries with its design-led platform. Both global brands as well as direct-to-consumer companies rely on its diverse services to reach customers daily. The company has been listed #1 in Deloitte's Fast 50 Central Europe 2020 ranking and as the most prominent startup in Europe by *Business Insider*.

[Funding History]

Pre-Seed   Seed

Packhelp raised €2.35 million ($2.7 million) over two seed rounds (in 2017 and 2018). The first was led by Movens Ventures and Kogito Ventures, and the second was raised from Speedinvest x, PROFounders and Market One Capital. In 2019, Packhelp raised €8.5 million ($10 million) in one of the largest Series A rounds in the CEE region, led by White Star Capital. In 2021, it raised 46.5 million in a Series B round.

[Milestones]

- Translating our apps and website to English and German while expanding abroad.
- Launching Packhelp Plus, a service for wholesale and tailor-made packaging, which allowed expansion to the mid-market.
- Investing in sustainable alternatives for all product ranges.
- Growing the company to two hundred employees and beginning to hire abroad.

[Links] Web: **packhelp.com** LinkedIn: **company/packhelp** Facebook: **packhelp**
Instagram: **@packhelp** Twitter: **@packhelpcom**

[Name] # Planet Heroes

[Elevator Pitch] *"We make people excited to clean up the environment. There is always some trash to pick up along the way. By sharing your work with a like-minded community, you can help keep the planet clean and get paid for it."*

[The Story] Planet Heroes, an eco-crowdfunding platform, was born out of the wish for a community dedicated to cleaning up the natural environment. As Planet Heroes, users can either help clean up an area (such as a forest or beach) or support others doing this work through donations. Users share the before and after pictures of the area and get cash in return. "There is always some trash wherever you go," says Karolina Gurgul, PR and communications manager at Planet Heroes, "so it helps when people can see results and receive financial motivation to clean it up." The assured five euros per every bag of collected trash guarantees users a just reward for their work. Karolina highlights a recent Zanzibar clean-up project whose proceeds help schools to buy new computers to further digital education in the Tanzanian capital. "It's a wonderful project that's showing a lot of results."

Planet Heroes is a UN partner and the official host of World Clean Up Day in Poland while also launching its official app later this year. "We had this original goal of collecting one million liters of trash when we started," says Karolina, "but what we ultimately want is to create a passion for cleaning up the planet. We want our heroes to share and be proud of their work."

[Funding History]

Bootstrap

Pre-Seed

External

Grants

Planet Heroes' initial funding came from the founders, but the project soon drew the attention of investors. After getting first place on the UN-Habitat Waste Wise City Campaign and the UN's Green Startup Marathon in Kenya, Planet Heroes went on to secure funding through the VC group Invento Capital.

[Milestones]

- Winning the UN Green Startup Marathon 2019 for distinguished community outreach.
- Launching Planet Heroes in Australia.
- Winning the 2019 Young Innovators Award from MIT EF CEE Acceleration Program.
- Becoming the official partner in Poland for World Clean Up Day 2021.

[Links] Web: planetheroes.app Facebook: PlanetHeroesApp Instagram: @planetheroes.official

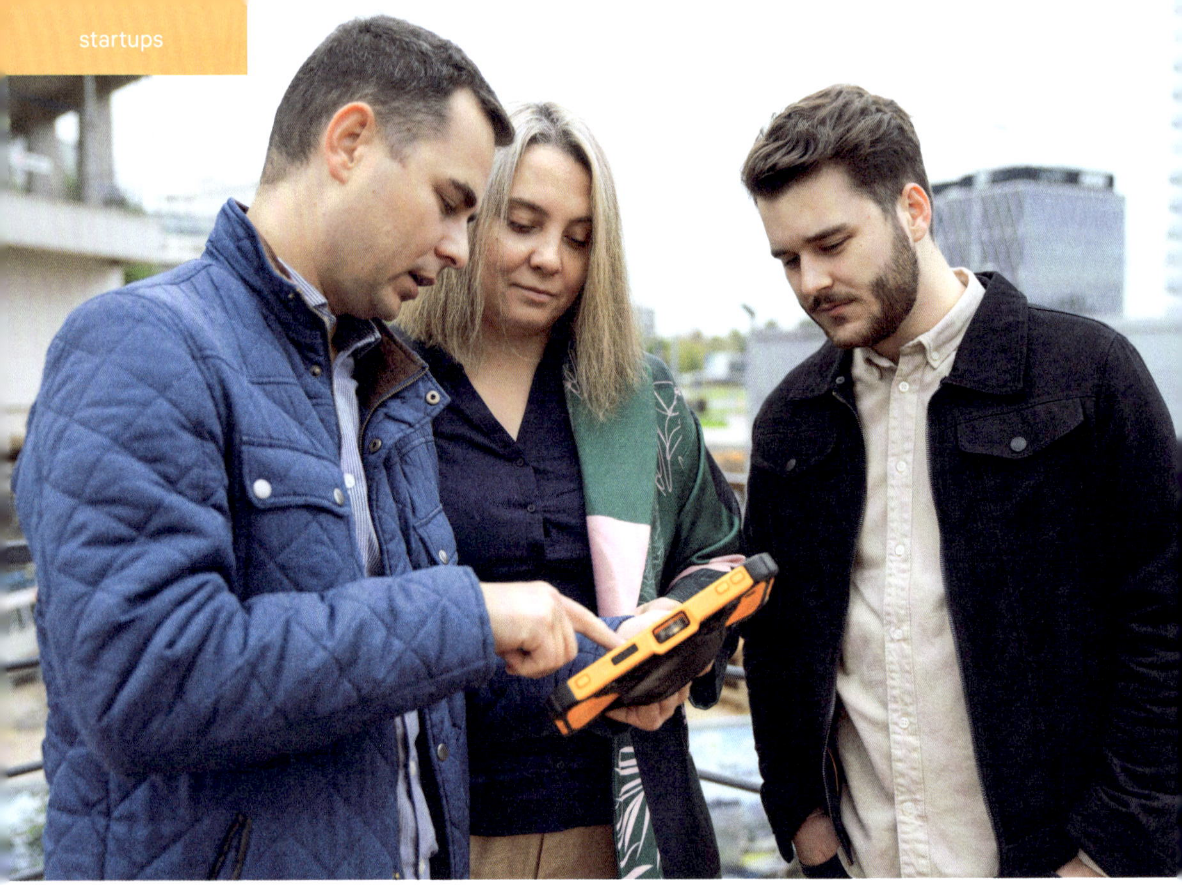

[Name]
ProperGate

[Elevator Pitch]

"We offer a smart delivery management system that offers real-time information and control of materials on construction sites."

[The Story]

ProperGate was founded in 2017 by a group of real estate, construction and technology professionals who observed how hefty the needs of one of their construction sites was. They needed a way to automate the processes and responsibilities at construction sites. The three founders and two early business angel investors held a shared vision of improving the way construction companies plan and implement logistics via digital technology. The company launched in January 2018, and within two years it became a globally awarded solution and was selected as a top contech (construction technology) company in rankings compiled by BuiltWorlds Chicago, REiN, Builtworld Germany, PwC, Cemex Ventures and BCG. It is also considered a rising star of ESG (environmental, social and corporate governance) by PwC, *Business Insider* and Ringier Axel Springer.

By giving site managers an interactive tool that helps them to save time on repeatable, time-consuming tasks, it allows them to focus on more important work and project decisions while increasing efficiency, improving safety and reducing wastage. The founders consider Warsaw a perfect environment for the company to thrive in, not only because it is a vibrant, modern metropolis with fast growing numbers of high-rise buildings being planned but also because the city acts as a good starting point for the localization of new investments.

[Funding History]

Pre-Seed   Seed

In 2021, ProperGate raised €1 million ($1.1 million) in a pre-seed round. Investors included leading international investment funds SMOK Ventures and Realty Corporation Limited and private investors with longstanding connections to the real estate industry. ProperGate is now raising its next investment round.

[Milestones]

- Finding business angels, investors and a dedicated team who helped brainstorm and deliver strategic decisions.
- Being able to scout ideal clients for pilot projects.
- Fueling the boom of the warehouse market by taking advantage of the post-pandemic market situation.
- Focusing on strengthening our domestic market as much as our international one.

[Links]

Web: propergate.co LinkedIn: company/propergate Facebook: ProperGateApp
Twitter: @propergateapp

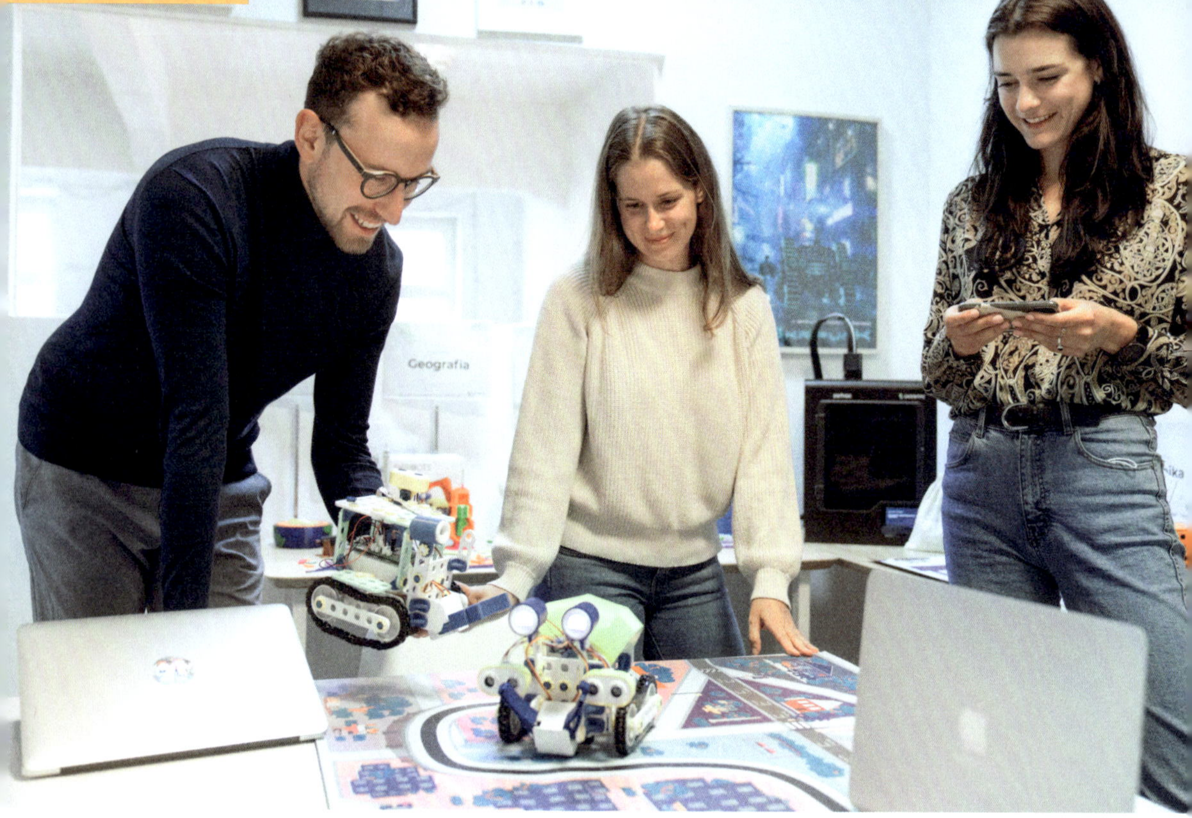
Geografia

Certificate

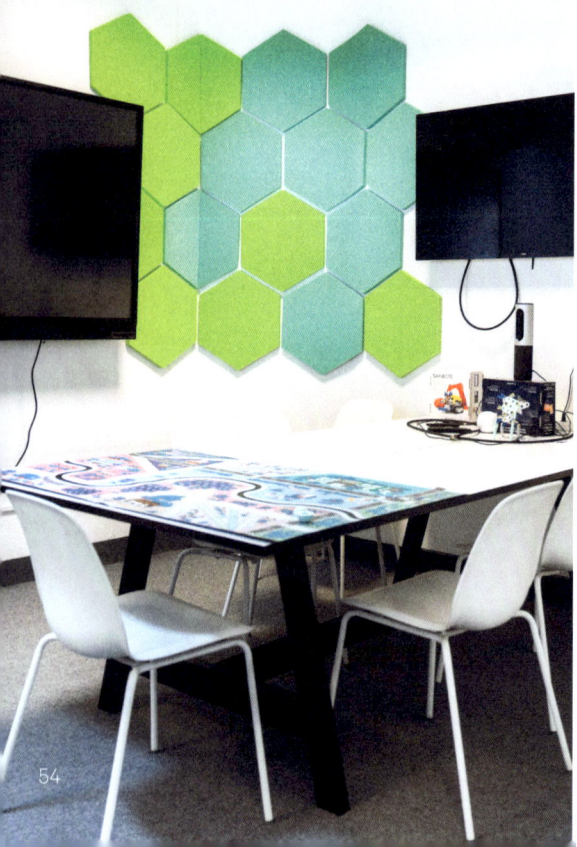

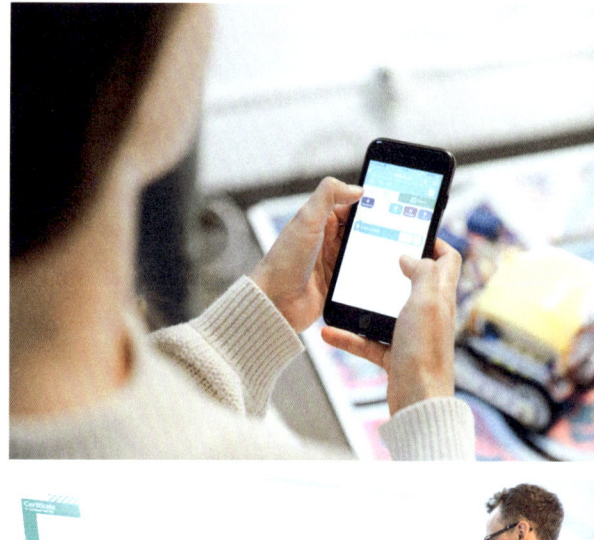

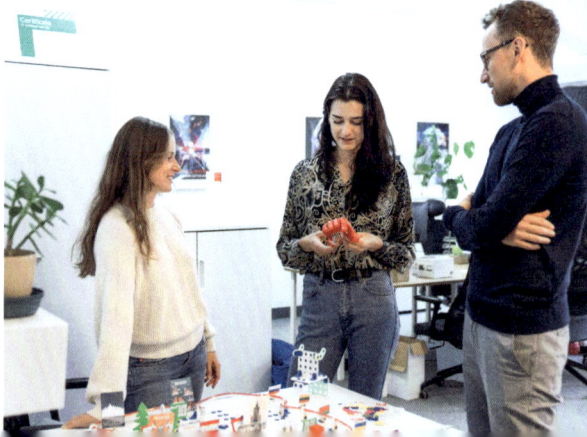

[Name] # Skriware

[Elevator Pitch] *"We've created an educational laboratory based on 3D print, robotics and programming suitable for all stages of K12 (primary) education."*

[The Story] Skriware is the bridge between science and creativity. Founded in 2015 by passionate individuals focused on robotics and 3D printing, the company initially set out to produce the first user-friendly 3D printer and later to popularize the technology. However, the founders soon identified a gap in the market: educators could use these technologies in their classrooms. Skriware created a fully integrated educational laboratory, the SkriLab, which uses modern tools, materials and teaching aids in accordance with the core curriculum of most school subjects. It has now become a comprehensive educational ecosystem covering the fields of 3D modeling and printing, robotics and engineering for schools that want to respond to the challenges of the modern world.

Skriware focuses on becoming a thriving system not only for students but also for teachers, enabling them to thrive at their work, pass on their knowledge more effectively and improve their own abilities, all while interacting in one, unique, integrated ecosystem. Since pivoting to becoming an educational ecosystem of products that focuses on developing practical skills and a creative approach to problem-solving, onboarding has become easier, while also opening a door to the regular use of technology in schools. The startup also offers tech support to teachers, helping them in the implementation and methodological oversight.

[Funding History]

Pre-Seed   Seed   Grants

Skriware's funding story can be divided into two types of funding: equity and grant (mostly R&D and sales grants) support. From 2017 till 2021, the company managed to collect almost €1.5 million ($1.8 million) from grants alone. They have also received support from individual business angels in 2020 and 2021 and are currently preparing for another private, pre-IPO round. By March 2022, they hope to become a joint-stock company.

[Milestones]

- Selecting a mix of passionate and brave engineers, innovators and creatives to join the team.
- Shifting the direction from being a 3D-printing company to an edtech startup.
- Surviving the 2020 pandemic, which eventually introduced radical changes to the education system (and thus, the startup).
- Receiving record-breaking funds that allowed us to continue investing in education.

[Links] Web: **skriware.com** LinkedIn: **company/skriware** Facebook: **Skriware**
Instagram: **@skriware** Twitter: **@Skriware**

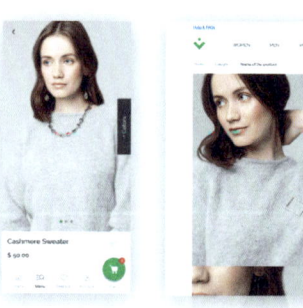
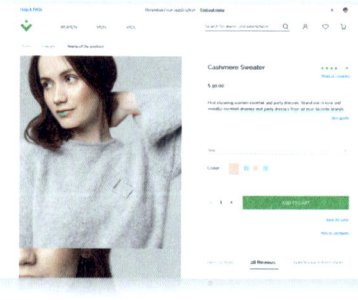

[Name]
Vue Storefront

[Elevator Pitch]

"Ecommerce companies are stuck on outdated legacy platforms and frontend solutions that are not optimized for today's users' expectations. We help companies to go headless faster, cheaper and better. We are the glue for headless commerce."

[The Story]

Vue Storefront provides developers with the needed technical solutions to keep up with the fast-growing ecommerce industry. The company is now the fastest-growing open-source project on GitHub. The idea for Vue Storefront emerged when the founders tried to solve a problem. In 2017, Patrick Friday and his colleagues were working for Divante, a global ecommerce-technology company, when they noticed that more and more users were migrating from desktop to mobile phones. Optimizing the software used back then did not achieve the needed results, because it meant higher costs for only slightly better performance. However, they realized that using Vue.js, a JavaScript library for building web interfaces, allowed for a remarkably improved experience for mobile users. They saw an opportunity for a new business using Vue.js for storefronts, which is where its name came from.

Headless ecommerce, which separates the front end of the store from the back end to improve flexibility, was relatively new when the company started out. The cofounders' biggest challenge was to convince investors of their idea. However, with the change of the demands of the market as many users migrated to mobile, investors began to develop an interest in the company to the point that Vue Storefront had one of the biggest Series A round in the history of Polish startups.

[Funding History]

Angel   Seed   External

In December 2020, Vue Storefront signed a VC seed round agreement and was accepted into Y Combinator. From January 2021, it started its journey as a company with seven employees. In its Series A funding round, it raised $17.5 million.

[Milestones]

- Deciding to spin off from Divante in 2019.
- Having customers from all over the world and going global from day one.
- Growing ten times in only nine months of operating.
- Having over seven hundred stores join Vue Storefront, including multi-billion-dollar revenue companies.

[Links]   **Web:** vuestorefront.io **LinkedIn:** company/vue-storefront **Facebook:** vuestorefront
Twitter: @VueStorefront

rams

- **Identify your resources.**
Find a team to support you. The first few months of starting a business are usually the hardest. Make sure you carefully identify the human or financial resources you have available to you so you can build a strong foundation.

- **Ask away.**
Don't be afraid to ask questions, especially in the beginning of the process. Problems that may arise as we get further in our collaborations can easily be avoided if you ask questions.

- **Know what you need.**
Do your research and find out what you'll need for your business. If you know what you need, it's easier to ask for it.

- **Have a strong *"why."***
Make sure to narrow down the reason behind the work you do. You're much more likely to succeed when you know why you do what you do.

[Name] # Akademickie Inkubatory Przedsiębiorczości (AIP)

[Elevator Pitch] *"We are a Polish program that strives to provide a legal identity and all the necessary tools to those who wish to fulfill their dream of creating their own business, regardless of their age or experience."*

[Sector] **Multiple**

[Description] Akademickie Inkubatory Przedsiębiorczości (AIP) is a Polish company with a mission to make its program "the most commonly used alternative to the traditional ways of starting a company," says Alicja Herda, startup manager at AIP. The program allows entrepreneurs to test out their business ideas without having to legally register their companies by themselves. AIP's clients receive accounting, HR and legal support as well as business consulting and mentoring. Additionally, the legal identity lent by the program provides safety and removes the burdens most commonly associated with starting your own company. The cost of the AIP program is 300 zł ($78) per month, and prospective clients can approach the program as early as the idea stage.

The program started in 2004 as the first ecosystem of its kind in Poland, with the initial goal of supporting university students with starting their own businesses. "At the beginning," says Alicja, "we were very local for many years." However, with the progress of technology over time, AIP was able to transition to a fully online program and provide the needed support to anyone in Poland, regardless of their location. Currently, more than seven hundred startups are supported by AIP. Some notable startups born at AIP include CallPage, a callback automation service that helps business owners connect with buyers faster; Plenti, the first mobile application in Poland offering on-demand electronic rentals; and Rendart, a graphic-design company specializing in marketing projects for the development industry.

AIP currently offers its services to two age groups: those under the age of twenty-six and those over. While the requirements and expectations of each age group are different, AIP's services all revolve around the fact that anyone should be able to realize their dreams and start their business. "Human creativity has no limit," says Alicja. "Anyone can join and start their company with us."

[Apply to] letsstartup@aip.link or aip.link

[Links] Web: aip.link LinkedIn: company/foundationakademickieinkubatoryprzedsiębiorczości
Facebook: AIPWorldOfStartups Instagram: @aip.link

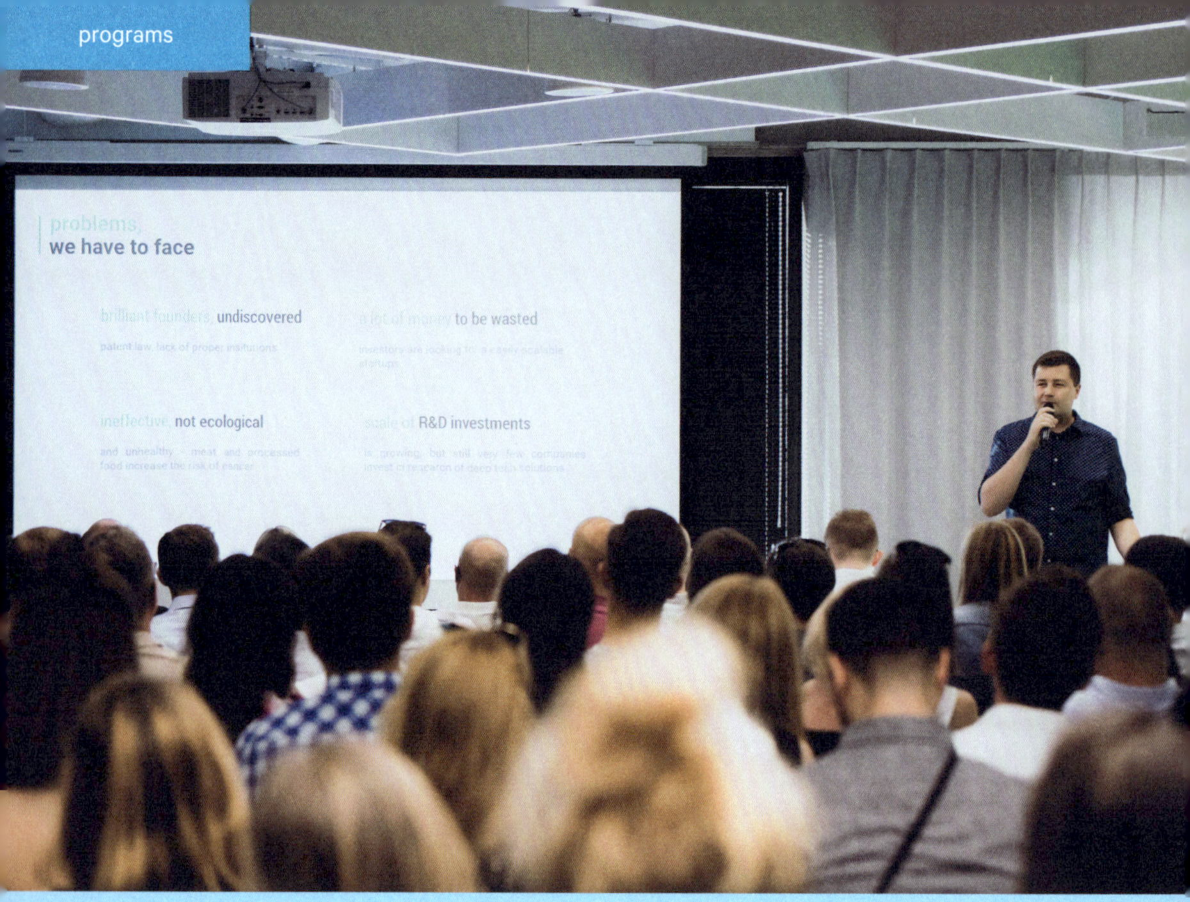

- **Don't hesitate to start working on your ideas.**
  The time is now. Bring your ideas to life and verify them with the market. The foodtech market has grown rapidly in the last two years, but it's still young. Now is the best moment to enter.

- **Verify, verify, verify.**
  Talk to your potential clients from the very beginning. That way, you can make sure the problem you're trying to solve is real and that your solution has a real chance for success.

- **Be focused.**
  You won't have a lot of resources, financial or human, at the beginning, so it's crucial to find the biggest pain points of your customers and focus on them.

- **Find your cofounder.**
  It's very hard to build a really big business by yourself, so think about building a team around you from the very beginning. This is a team sport.

[Name] # foodtech.ac

[Elevator Pitch] *"We are an accelerator program that supports and helps scale startups that aim to change the agrifood sector for the better. We provide mentorship and help with expanding your business network, receiving funding and more."*

[Sector] **agrifood, foodtech**

[Description] With the world moving more and more towards greener solutions, some wish to change the traditional business approach that dominates today and instead show how successful planet-friendly solutions can be. fooodtech.ac is among those driven by a vision to help save the planet, and it is bridging technology and food to accomplish that. The end-to-end, eight-week-long accelerator program prepares startups for entering the market and scaling. During every application period, only five or six truly promising and planet-friendly projects qualify for the program. This not only ensures an individual approach but allows space for the exploration of ideas and possibilities.

Most of the program's workshops, meetings and sessions with mentors take place two days a week. However, there are shorter activities on other days in addition to weekly personal meetings designed to guide the process and help with any ongoing issues. Startups are connected to relevant members of the foodtech.ac network such as corporations, scientists and experienced entrepreneurs. The official part of the program ends with a demo day where the startups present their solutions to an audience of investors and press. However, the support of the program does not end there. "We remain in touch with our alumni and help them further their development and funding," says Małgorzata Żurowska, the project manager at foodtech.ac. Some notable alumni include Apollo, a plant-based chicken alternative sold all over Poland; It's Bean, a protein-packed, plant-based yogurt alternative; and Listny Cud, a vertical-farming startup, the first in Poland to introduce in-store vertical farms in a major supermarket chain. While the program is mainly interested in projects with a prototype of a finished product, it is open to other stages as well, says Małgorzata. "If you have a promising team and just a revolutionary idea, let's talk."

[Apply to] info@foodtech.ac or foodtech.ac

[Links] Web: **foodtech.ac** LinkedIn: **company/foodtechac** Facebook: **foodtechac**
Instagram: **@foodtech.ac**

- **Have an MVP.**
  Be at the stage where we can test your products
  and where you have a deep understanding of your
  target market and potential competition.

- **Have a solid founding team.**
  We do not look for individuals but for teams. Your
  team is very important for the success of your
  business. We want you all to be motivated to
  succeed and have shared values with not only your
  team but with the corporate partners we work with.

- **Be able to receive feedback, and be open to being
  mentored and coached.**
  Our aim is to help you reach your potential, but you
  must be receptive and open to learning.

- **Have innovative minds and ideas.**
  We are looking for completely unique and individual
  ideas. We get excited about solutions that solve
  truly tricky worldwide problems – not just the
  problems of today, but of tomorrow.

[Name]
Foundation for Technology Entrepreneurship

[Elevator Pitch]
"We are a startup-acceleration program affiliated with MIT and aimed at ambitious and innovative startups. Through our rigorous and highly regarded program, we help early-stage startups to thrive and grow, connecting them with corporate partners and investors."

[Sector]
Sector agnostic

[Description]
In 2015, Bogy Skowronski, Paweł Bochniarz and Krzysztof Gawrysiak joined together to bridge the knowledge, skills and network gap they saw in Poland's startup sector. Combining their years of experience across sectors and their desire to support CEE startups to scale internationally, they set up the Foundation for Technology Entrepreneurship. It is one of the first Polish organizations to enable corporations and large organizations to work closely with startups. Through its work and expansive network, the foundation guides both corporates and startups, acting as a connector and matchmaker. It helps large organizations to collaborate with startups and facilitates the building of mutually beneficial relationships. It also oversees and collaborates on a range of accelerator and innovation programs. The foundation was a partner on the MassChallenge International Accelerator Program and previously worked on the SmartUp Accelerator. It also operates the MIT (Massachusetts Institute of Technology) Enterprise Forum Accelerator in the CEE area and plans to build innovation hubs in the region.

The foundation's flagship project is the acceleration program aimed at the most innovative startups in the CEE area and recognized by and affiliated with MIT. The first edition, held in 2016, was aimed at deep-tech startups. It now takes place twice annually and offers a diverse range of open calls from industry that startups can apply to. The program consists of six core areas: workshops, mentoring sessions, proof-of-concept meetings in collaboration with corporate partners, pitching sessions, a demo day and a final bootcamp for the winners of the demo day. A fundamental part of the program is the workshop series, based on the twenty-four-step startup methodology by Prof. Bill Aulet from MIT called Disciplined Entrepreneurship. During the rigorous and intensive program, startups have the opportunity to collaborate with international corporate partners, present to a broad range of potential investors and join the foundation's elite alumni club.

[Apply to]
mitefcee.org/accelerator

[Links]
Web: mitefcee.org LinkedIn: company/mit-enterprise-forum-poland-technology-entrepreneurship-foundation- Facebook: MITEFCEE

- **Be based in the area where we operate.**
  We focus on startups in Poland and Europe.

- **Have a ready product.**
  A ready product helps us access your project
  and your ability to attract customers.

- **Have a minimum of ten to fifteen people
  in the team.**
  Your team must be willing to dedicate time for
  different mentoring sessions and workshops.

- **Ensure your sector meets the criteria
  of the program.**
  The sectors we target vary from one program
  to another. Make sure your product matches the
  field the program addresses in each round.

[Name]
Google for Startups

[Elevator Pitch]
"We connect startups with the right people, products and best practices to help them grow."

[Sector]
Growth-stage startups (any sector)

[Description]
Google for Startups in Warsaw offers two different types of programs: Startup School and high-touch programs. The Startup School functions as an entry point for startups in which they participate in short workshops about Google products such as Google Ads, Google Analytics and Google Cloud. The high-touch programs – the Founders Academy, Founders Academy: Women Founders, Growth Academy and Google for Startups Accelerator: Europe – are more advanced long-term programs (three months) and offered to a small, selected group of startups. These programs target any growth-stage startup from any sector. However, some editions of the programs are focused on a specific field or a group of founders. For example, in 2021, the healthtech and well-being sector was chosen for the Google for Startups Accelerator: Europe program. Participating startups are focused on improving health and well-being (fighting burnout, anxiety, depression) in order to disrupt and thus improve health systems around the planet.

High-touch programs offer help with technological challenges, connect startups with mentors and experts in the field from within and outside Google, and address the needs of each startup. They help startups to scale and show them how to expand internationally and acquire new users. The programs also share Google's best practices and know-how; for example, how to implement the OKR (objectives and key results) framework.

One startup that benefited greatly from Google for Startups was Infermedica, which the program helped accelerate through mentoring sessions and workshops on Google products. Infermedica now operates in thirty countries and managed to increase its team from 90 to 180 people. Founders Academy: Women Founders, which is open for women from Poland, Germany, Austria and Switzerland, focuses on women's leadership skills, helps participants to concretize their vision and mission, and stresses the importance of becoming a leader who inspires rather than becoming a manager.

[Apply to]
campus.co/warsaw/programs

[Links]
Web: campus.co/warsaw/programs LinkedIn: showcase/google-for-startups
Facebook: GoogleForStartups Instagram: @googleforstartups Twitter: @GoogleStartups

- **Technology should be at the heart of what you do.**
  We are looking to support startups who have
  technology at the core of what they do and who are
  developing a software-based product or service.

- **Be committed.**
  The startups we work with must be committed
  to working with Microsoft. We facilitate many
  opportunities to use our solutions and platforms
  but you must be willing to learn and grow.

- **Have an international outlook.**
  We want you to think globally, not just locally,
  and to reflect that in your brand presence and
  market focus.

- **Your idea needs to be innovative.**
  We want to see startups and companies who
  are truly innovative, offer something completely
  different, and solve a genuine problem.

- **Be scalable.**
  We want to see that your offer is not only
  technologically advanced but also has the potential
  to be scaled.

[Name] # Microsoft for Startups

[Elevator Pitch] *"We help remove traditional barriers to building a tech company by democratizing resources, expert mentorship and access to capital. Get started on the platform and gain free access to the technology and support you need to turn your dream into a life-changing product."*

[Sector] **Software**

[Description] Microsoft for Startups is a free global support and educational program offered to all founders who want to scale and grow their business. Through Microsoft for Startups Founders Hub, it offers startups access to powerful Microsoft cloud tools and technology and provides a range of opportunities for them to engage and participate in Microsoft's global network and ecosystem. Participating companies are awarded up to $150,000 in credits to spend on Azure (Microsoft's cloud technology) and are also given access to Github and Microsoft Teams to help them expand their business. Microsoft for Startups also provides technical advisory sessions to help startups build at every stage. Each startup has the chance to attend educational workshops and receive tailored advice as well as unique content. For late-stage startups ready to scale across the world through the Azure Marketplace and appsource – Microsoft's online marketplace for business applications and solutions – the startups are given a one-of-a-kind opportunity to promote and market themselves directly to customers.

The program is open to any startup in Poland that is both reliant on and a high consumer of cloud technology, and that needs technical solutions to kickstart its business growth. Eligible startups can apply directly through the website.

Microsoft for Startups provides entrepreneurs with the resources and mentorship they need to run and build their business. Its one-of-a-kind program supports founders from idea to exit through a range of opportunities, including matching startups with Microsoft experts to help bring their business to life, offering support building technology solutions that will help startups to grow, and running exclusive educational workshops that are offered to all participants.

[Apply to] startups.microsoft.com

[Links] Web: **startups.microsoft.com** LinkedIn: **company/microsoftforstartups**
Facebook: **Microsoft4Startups** Twitter: **@msft4startups**

- Be a registered company in Warsaw or the Mazovian district.
  You must be Poland-based to apply.

- Represent a micro-enterprise or startup.
  That is, at least in the refinement or scaling phase (have a minimum one to two years in the market or be currently expanding or in the pivoting process).

- Represent a sector that was hit during the COVID-19 pandemic.
  Startups in retail, hospitality and services take precedence, as these fields experienced a significant decrease in revenue during the pandemic.

- Be largely female led in some capacity.
  Whether that is by having a female founder or cofounder, or where women employees make up at least 50 percent.

[Name]

NEXT Acceleration Program For Female Founders

[Elevator Pitch]

"We are a one-year educational training, business mentoring and networking program for female founders who have decided to scale up and internationalize their enterprises."

[Sector]

Female-owned micro-enterprises and SMEs

[Description]

The NEXT Acceleration Program For Female Founders targets female founders whose companies are ready to grow. It provides one year of educational training, business mentoring and networking sessions with other female entrepreneurs. The program, which was created and organized by Female Entrepreneurship Foundation with support of JP Morgan, considers itself an MBA, for all intents and purposes, but for business owners. It is the first, and now one of the top, accelerator programs for female founders in Warsaw's startup ecosystem.

Seven years prior to founding NEXT, its founders were offering an acceleration program called Business in Women's Hands for future female founders. During the eight-month program, they taught founders how to start a business and lead it with a business plan. Since the first Business in Women's Hands edition, almost three hundred female-owned businesses were able to grow and scale up, both in the Polish and global market. After years of incubating early-stage female startups, the founders saw the needs of the women involved to keep growing, expand internationally and continue to digitize and innovate. Thus, NEXT was born.

NEXT's ultimate goal is to encourage more women leaders who aspire to scale up and bring their business onto the global stage while building new contacts, strengthening self-awareness of their own competencies and breaking down barriers for women founders in unique industries. During the program, all participants are offered an initial diagnosis of their enterprises' business potential along with different educational paths that focus on either digital transformation, innovation or networking. Within the program, mentors and expert consultants discuss strategy ideas, legal issues and any business challenges that may arise. Workshops and demo days are also included within the program.

[Apply to] siecprzedsiebiorczychkobiet.pl/next

[Links] Web: siecprzedsiebiorczychkobiet.pl LinkedIn: company/fundacja-przedsiebiorczosci-kobiet
Facebook: SiecPrzedsiebiorczychKobiet Instagram: @siecprzedsiebiorczychkobiet

- **Be a team player.**
  Our program is based on teamwork and mutual development. So if you do not thrive in a team-based environment, then our program is not for you.

- **Have a strong *why*.**
  During our selection process, we look for participants that show great potential in becoming tech entrepreneurs. Be sure to find your why, and be certain of your ideas.

- **Prepare to commit.**
  Our workshops are intensive and require your full involvement. Make sure that you are ready to make this commitment to your growth and success.

- **Be ready for a challenge-based education.**
  We offer our participants practical and hands-on education. Make sure that that is what you are looking for.

[Name]

PFR School of Pioneers

[Elevator Pitch]

"We are an international educational program dedicated to future tech entrepreneurs and visionaries. Our venture-builder is designed to boost your competence with key business skills, international collaboration and networking, and tech know-how."

[Sector]

Technology

[Description]

Founded in 2018, the PFR School of Pioneers is an international program designed by the Polish Development Fund and Allegro to help accelerate aspiring tech entrepreneurs. For three weeks in September, participants take part in intensive workshops held in Warsaw and conducted by experienced professionals, large technological companies, and successful startups and experts in the innovative sectors. The cost of admission is 500 zł ($130), and the program focuses on connecting individuals from different backgrounds, including business, science, technology and creative, and guiding them into interdisciplinary teams to build scalable, innovative solutions. The workshops are highly practical and challenge-based and include weekly trainings on team-building, the financial ins and outs of new companies, marketing, PR and the perfect investor presentation. The first week of the program focuses on personal development and team building, and the second and third weeks on market validation and prototyping, sales, marketing and financing.

After the conclusion of the workshops, founding teams continue to develop their projects with the support of mentors for several weeks until the Final Gala. The best teams will qualify for an additional training in one of the European ecosystems, and three winners will receive financial awards. The goal of international training is for participants to gain knowledge on the ecosystem, validate their unique projects and receive additional support. The PFR School of Pioneers looks for aspiring entrepreneurs aged twenty to forty who are working on honing their skills in the technology sector and are determined to develop their own businesses.

Some notable companies that have advanced their journey with support from the School of Pioneers include VividQ, the world's first complete power platform for full holographic 3D display; Unicorn VR World, a platform that creates a novel approach to therapy for children on the autism spectrum using VR; and HearMe, a platform supporting the mental health of employees by offering online therapy, webinars and workshops.

[Apply to]

startup.pfr.pl/en/pfr-school-pioneers

[Links]

Web: startup.pfr.pl/en LinkedIn: school/pfr-school-of-pioneers Facebook: PFRInnowacje Twitter: @PFRInnowacje

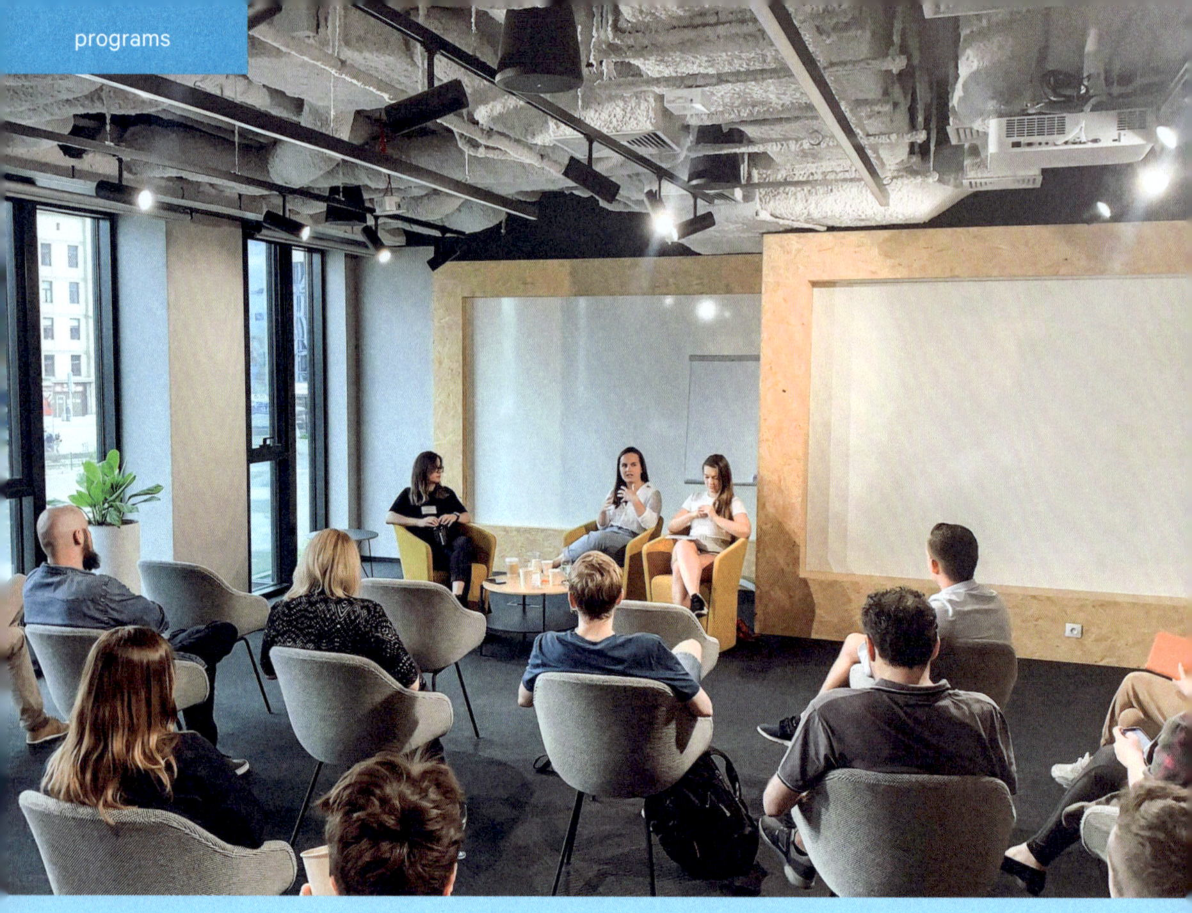

- **Understand your industry.**
  We want you to be really knowledgeable and excited about the industry you work in. The program is very intense, so you must be ready to work hard and to become an expert in what you do.

- **Have a strong founding team.**
  We want your team to be really strong and to possess a broad range of skills that will help make your business a success.

- **Be ready to test your business idea.**
  Our aim is to support you to realize your ideas and dreams and make them a success, so be prepared to be challenged.

- **Be willing to join the global stage.**
  We want your scope to go beyond the local market and for you to think about the global potential of your business.

[Name] # ReaktorX

[Elevator Pitch] *"We are one of the leading programs in the CEE region that supports first-time founders and early-stage startups. We work with them to develop their ideas and prepare for their first funding round or first big client."*

[Sector] **Sector agnostic**

[Description] As one of the first acceleration programs in Poland, ReaktorX initially grew out of ReaktorWarsaw, a startup hub with a lively community, monthly events, mentoring sessions and coworking space. ReaktorWarsaw was founded in 2011 by three of Poland's leading startup experts, Borys Musielak, Ania Walkowska and Kuba Filipowski. Having experienced what it was like to run a business, they wanted to open their doors to others and share the lessons they had learned. In 2016, Diana Koziarska joined ReaktorWarsaw, and together with Borys Musielak cofounded ReaktorX acceleration program, with the aim to support early-stage startups in the CEE region.

ReaktorX supports founders to go from idea to first funding. During the program, participants take part in online workshops, one-to-one sessions with their lead mentor and other ReaktorX mentors, networking events and pitching sessions in preparation for the demo day. At the demo day, which is attended by representatives from across the startup ecosystem, all startups have the chance to pitch their business idea. A jury of experts chooses three overall winners, who receive a targeted marketing and PR campaign and access to the ReaktorX network of potential investors. Following the program, all startups can choose to continue working with their mentor and have access to a wealth of resources. While the new team is managing ReaktorX, Borys and Diana, along with Paul and Dan Bragiel, cofounded SMOK Ventures, a US-Polish venture capital fund that invests in early stage startups in the CEE region. They still support the program as advisors and mentors.

[Apply to] app.vestbee.com/org/reaktor

[Links] Web: reaktorx.com LinkedIn: company/reaktorx Facebook: ReaktorWarsaw
Twitter: @ReaktorWarsaw

- **Be ambitious yet humble.**
  Be hungry to grow and succeed. It goes without saying that you need to be ambitious, but we want you to be humble when receiving feedback and open to rethinking key principles of your business.

- **Have an evenly balanced team.**
  Bring a broad and varied skill set to the table. You need to show that your collective experience encompasses a diverse range of areas and that you are also aware of the gaps in knowledge.

- **Have a unique product or business.**
  Business models can be copied easily, but unique products and technology can and must be protected.

- **Get ready to test your product.**
  We want you to test, test and test your product. We will put you through your paces to make sure that your product and business has a viable and sustainable future and the potential to grow exponentially.

[Name]
Startup Hub Poland

[Elevator Pitch]
"We help the most disruptive and innovative pioneers across the CEE region to engage with outstanding Polish opportunities and organizations. We offer exceptional advice, multiple programs and unparalleled connections to help your startup thrive in Poland and beyond."

[Sector]
Technology, acceleration

[Description]
In 2012, a group of Polish investors, startup founders and innovation brokers – Marek Borzetowski, Zygmunt Grajkowski, Robert Dziubłowski, Marek Trojanowicz and Maciej Sadowski – saw an opportunity to create a startup hub in Poland. Their ultimate goal was to create a one-stop-shop for startups and innovators in the CEE region, offering organizations and individuals the resources, expertise and network to expand and become competitors on the global stage. Since its inception, the Startup Hub Poland's offering has evolved from collaborative initiatives with a select network of partners into in-house programs and one-to-one assistance. It has also built an unparalleled network and community that helps give companies the best possible start when launching or scaling their businesses. With connections across the globe, it also serves as a signposting and matchmaking service, connecting companies and investors and building a pipeline of businesses for a worldwide audience.

Throughout the year, the Hub adapts and develops its partnerships and programs according to demand and market need. One long-standing program it has overseen and managed is the Warsaw Booster. Working with the City of Warsaw, the free acceleration program is offered to young and ambitious startups and founders in the tech industry. In 2018 and 2019, the Hub was also responsible for the pilot program by the Polish Agency for Enterprise Development (PARP) called the Poland Prize, which helped teams from outside of the CEE region to expand into those markets. Twenty-six new companies were incorporated in Poland following this initiative. In 2020, the Hub worked with the Polish Investment and Trade Agency, PARP, and GOVTECH on the Poland Business Harbour program, which helped Belarusian teams to develop their businesses through financial and expert support. Having built a solid network and ecosystem within Poland and beyond, the Hub is uniquely positioned to act as a conduit and conductor for startups with global ambitions.

[Apply to]
startuphub.pl

[Links]
Web: startuphub.pl LinkedIn: company/startup-hub-poland-foundation
Facebook: StartUpHubPoland Twitter: @HubSHP

- **Run or intend to run one's own business in Warsaw.**
  You should be running companies or startup projects no more than three years old.

- **Involve products or services that are based on technology.**
  For example, we're looking for startups based on AI, IoT, big data analysis, cloud computing, VR or AR.

- **Be open to external knowledge.**
  We focus heavily on networking, direct relations with the community, and active listening to and learning from other participants, experts and mentors in the program.

- **Aim to accelerate based on the Individual Acceleration Track already provided.**
  Activities, knowledge and supporting mentors, advisors and partners are then individually matched to your startup profile, if you qualify.

[Name] # Warsaw Booster

[Elevator Pitch] *"We are the only urban startup acceleration program for new technology projects in Poland. Our goal is to support young technology startups in improving their business competencies."*

[Sector] **urban dwelling, various**

[Description] Warsaw Booster is an annual municipal acceleration program that supports startups focused on developing innovative technological solutions and improving business competencies. The program provides opportunities to scale the business and acquire financing, and create unique business relationships. Since 2015, several hundred project teams have benefited from this free-of-charge support. Every edition of the program is run by a nonprofit organization with experience supporting innovation.

Participants admitted to the program receive individual support tailored to their individual needs from advisors and mentors from large international corporations, key NGOs, significant Polish companies, municipal businesses and local government entities. Their individualized acceleration model makes it possible for the program operators to respond to the diverse needs of all the different startups involved. Those encouraged to apply are mainly ambitious entrepreneurs interested in support tailored to their current business needs and eager to exchange experiences and networking contacts. The success of Warsaw Booster is evident from not only the large number of partners willing to cooperate and support startups in the program but also the increasing number of participants applying every year. As a part of this year's program, startups were awarded prizes worth over 85,000 zł ($23,000), with this year's theme involving high-tech solutions, products or services sought to improve the quality of life of residents and visitors to the capital. Among the participants are projects that support the local administration and other municipal companies. These startups advise on task implementation and on responses to challenges related to the sustainable development of the city as well as on contributions geared toward mitigating climate change. In the past, applicants have applied with topics related to design, fashion, smart city, financial or insurance services. Next editions will be focused on startups offering innovative solutions to specific municipal challenges.

[Apply to] warsawbooster21.pl/p,1,o-programie

[Links] Web: warsawbooster21.pl Facebook: warsawbooster Instagram: @warsawbooster
Twitter: @warsawbooster

spa

ces

[Name] # The Brain Embassy

[Address] Adgar Park West, al. Jerozolimskie 181B, 02-222 Warsaw

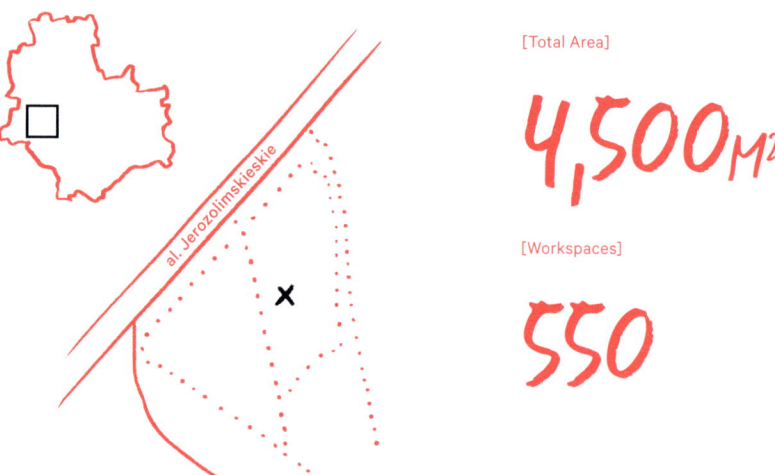

[Total Area]

4,500m²

[Workspaces]

550

[The Story] The Brain Embassy, a coworking space with multiple locations in Poland, Belgium and Israel, is owned by Adgar Investments and Development Ltd, an Israel-based company active in the real estate sector. The first Brain Embassy location was built in Warsaw within the context of rising popularity and demand for coworking spaces in Poland. However, the Brain Embassy team was not satisfied with merely building a coworking space and instead wished to create a community committed to cocreation. "It is very important for us to get to know each other, exchange knowledge and cocreate," says Global Brand and Experience Manager Iwona Barszcz. "We are a big family, and together we build a story."

At Brain Embassy Jerozolimskie, everyone can find a unique space that is right for them, as individual needs and team sizes are accommodated. The location offers an open space, private offices, company units and private units, as well as meeting, workshop and conference spaces. The space also offers 24/7 access, parking spaces, meditation and nap rooms, and a fully equipped kitchen and showers. It's pet friendly and requires only a one-month cancellation notice from its members. The space's own program, Be Smarter Together, also schedules monthly yoga classes, English lessons, consultancy hours and even concerts for its members.

[Links] Web: brainembassy.com LinkedIn: company/brainembassy Facebook: brainembassy
Instagram: brainembassy_warsaw

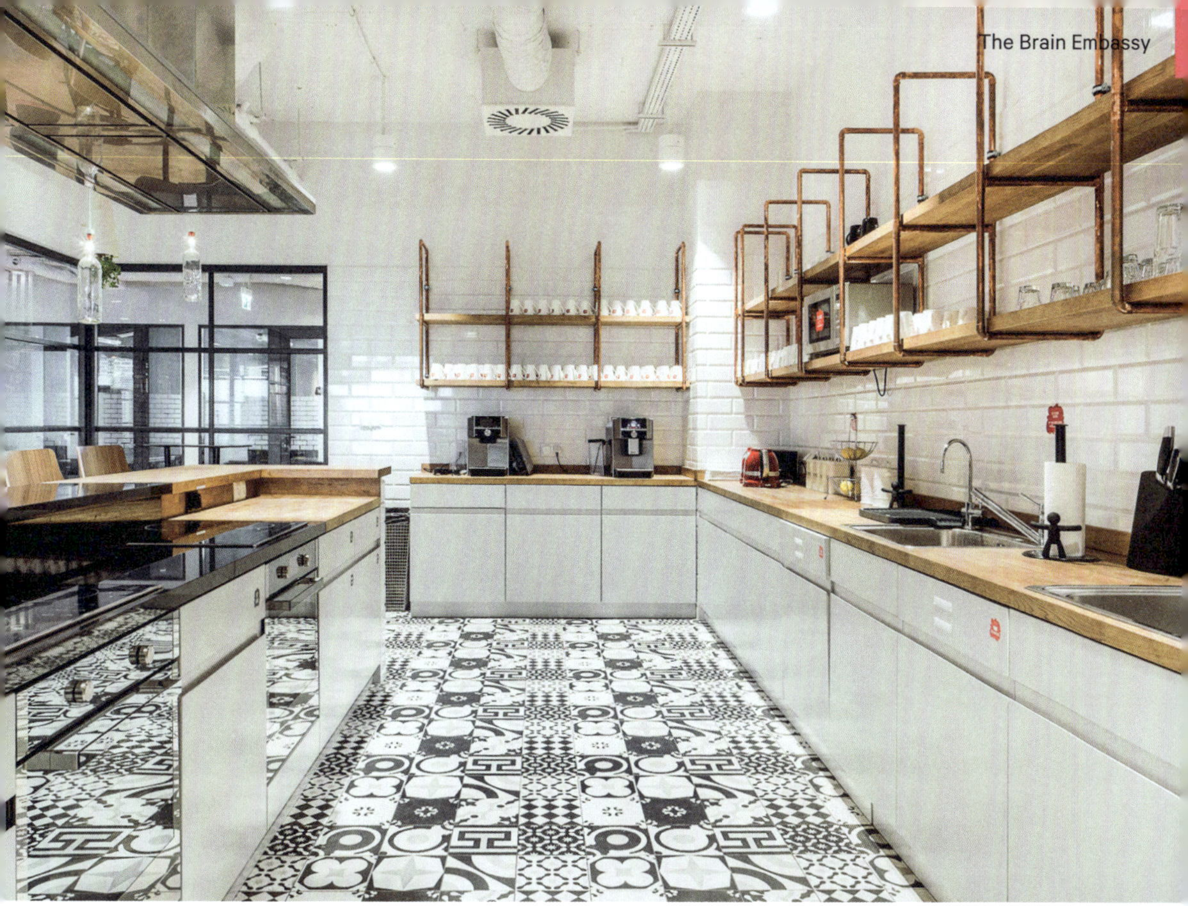

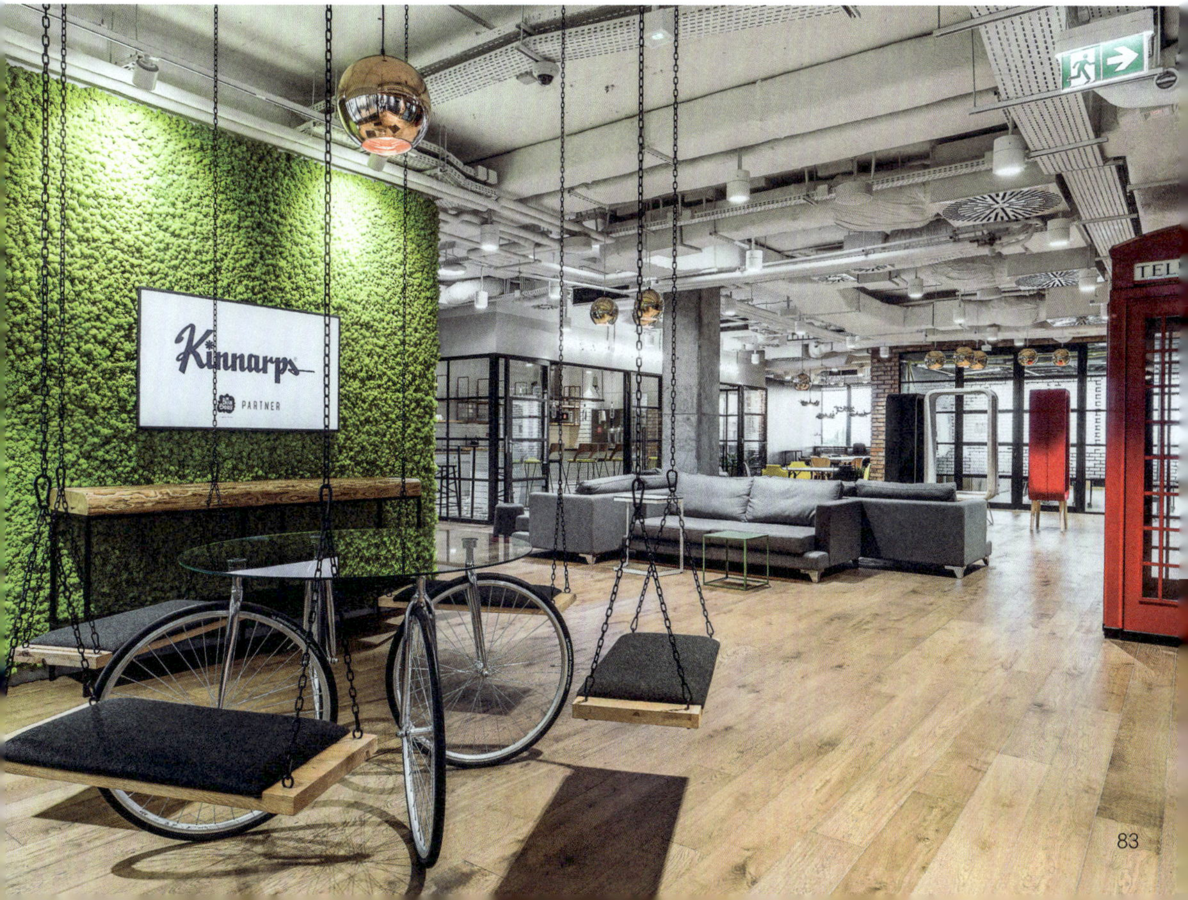
Kinnarps
PARTNER

Face of the Space:

Monika Kaczmarczyk has been working for Adgar Poland for ten years and is the cocreator of the Brain Embassy coworking space, a first of its kind in Poland. The space was created based on the latest global trends in designing functional, ergonomic and creative workspaces. The Brain Embassy, implemented and managed by Monika Kaczmarczyk, has become a coworking space setting trends on the market and winning prestigious national and international awards.

[Name] # Centrum Kreatywności Targowa

[Address] ul. Targowa 56, 03-733 Warsaw

[Total Area]

5,000m²

[Workspaces]

33

[The Story] Centrum Kreatywności Targowa (Targowa Creativity Centre) was brought to life by Warsaw City Hall in 2016. In 2019, for the first time in the history of Warsaw the City Hall entered into partnership with a private-sector organization by allowing the Polish Chamber of Commerce to run the center. The partnership will last till 2029. Due to the longevity of the partnership agreement, Centrum Kreatywności Targowa team members believe that many projects could be developed in their space over the coming years. One major difficulty for Centrum Kreatywności Targowa launching in 2019 was the pandemic, meaning many businesses moved to work from home. However, as the situation developed, coworking spaces observing safety measures were allowed in Warsaw while traditional office spaces remained closed. Centrum Kreatywności Targowa became a home for many companies that needed a base during lockdown.

There are currently over twenty companies using the space, representing a diverse range of sectors. Around nine companies are from the creative sector. The space houses over one hundred people daily, with startup offices, a conference space of 580 m² and an exhibition hall. It offers free training, mentoring and networking opportunities with experts in various fields. The team is especially passionate about the expert workshops on sustainable development and environmental protection they provide to several resident companies.

[Links] Web: cktargowa.pl LinkedIn: company/cktargowa Facebook: CKTargowa

Face of the Space:

Ewa Janus-Khouri (CEO Targowa Creativity Centre) has been a part of the Polish Chamber of Commerce for many years. Throughout her career, she has been devoted to the development of Polish entrepreneurship in cooperation with representatives of business, local government, public administration and NGOs. She is a manager and a coordinator of the Innovative Economy Congress and Young Innovative Congress. She is also a creator of communication and marketing projects and strategies as well as information campaigns.

[Name] # CIC Warsaw (Cambridge Innovation Center Warsaw)

[Address] Varso Place, Chmielna 73, 00-801 Warsaw

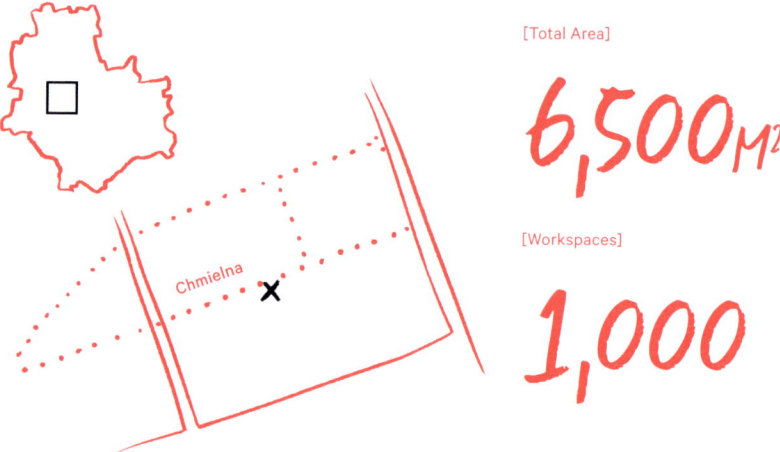

[Total Area]

6,500M²

[Workspaces]

1,000

Chmielna

[The Story] Founded in 1999 by Tim Rowe, the first Cambridge Innovation Center (CIC) started as an incubator in Massachusetts, where Tim and his colleagues could share ideas and office space. Over twenty years later, CIC is one of the oldest global hybrid office space providers and innovation communities. In June 2020, it opened CIC Warsaw in the Varso Place complex, which is next to the Central Railway Station and home to Varso Tower, the largest skyscraper in the European Union.

With its Innovation Campus, CIC Warsaw has created a pioneering way of working that includes flexible office space and multiple opportunities to engage with the wider startup ecosystem. The space is offered on flexible monthly terms with all-inclusive fees and has exceptional facilities such as multiple breakout spaces and meeting rooms, a wellness zone, game rooms, a parents room and a Prototyping Terrace with 3D printers operated by Sygnis S.A. CIC Warsaw also runs three innovation hubs (Internet of Everything Hub, Proptech Hub and Cosmic Hub), which together with leaders in each sector build communities around specific sectors of technology. All members have access to the global CIC network as well as District Hall, a free coworking and event space managed by the Venture Café Warsaw Foundation. The campus is also home to Trend House, a members club for high-impact leaders.

[Links] Web: cic.com/en/warsaw LinkedIn: company/cicwarsaw Facebook: cicwarsaw Instagram: cic_warsaw

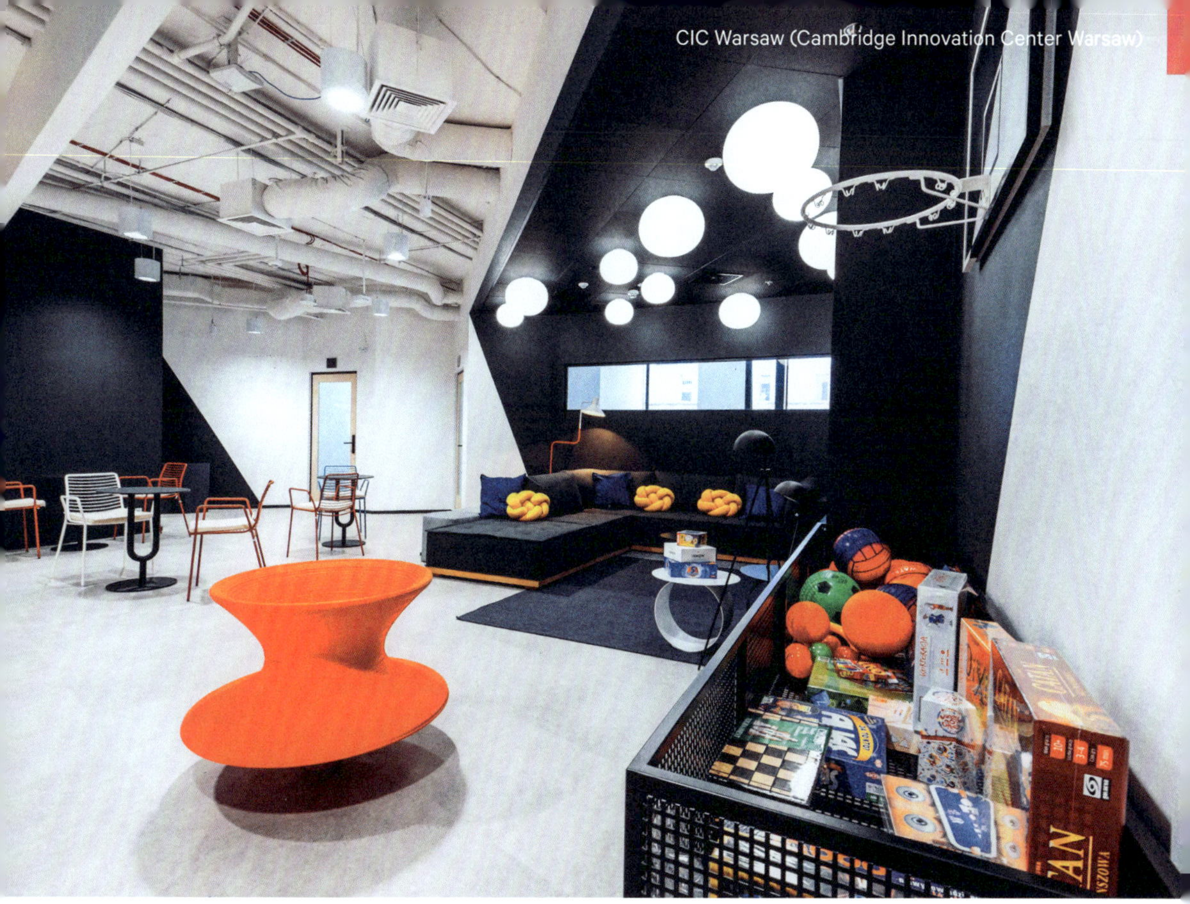

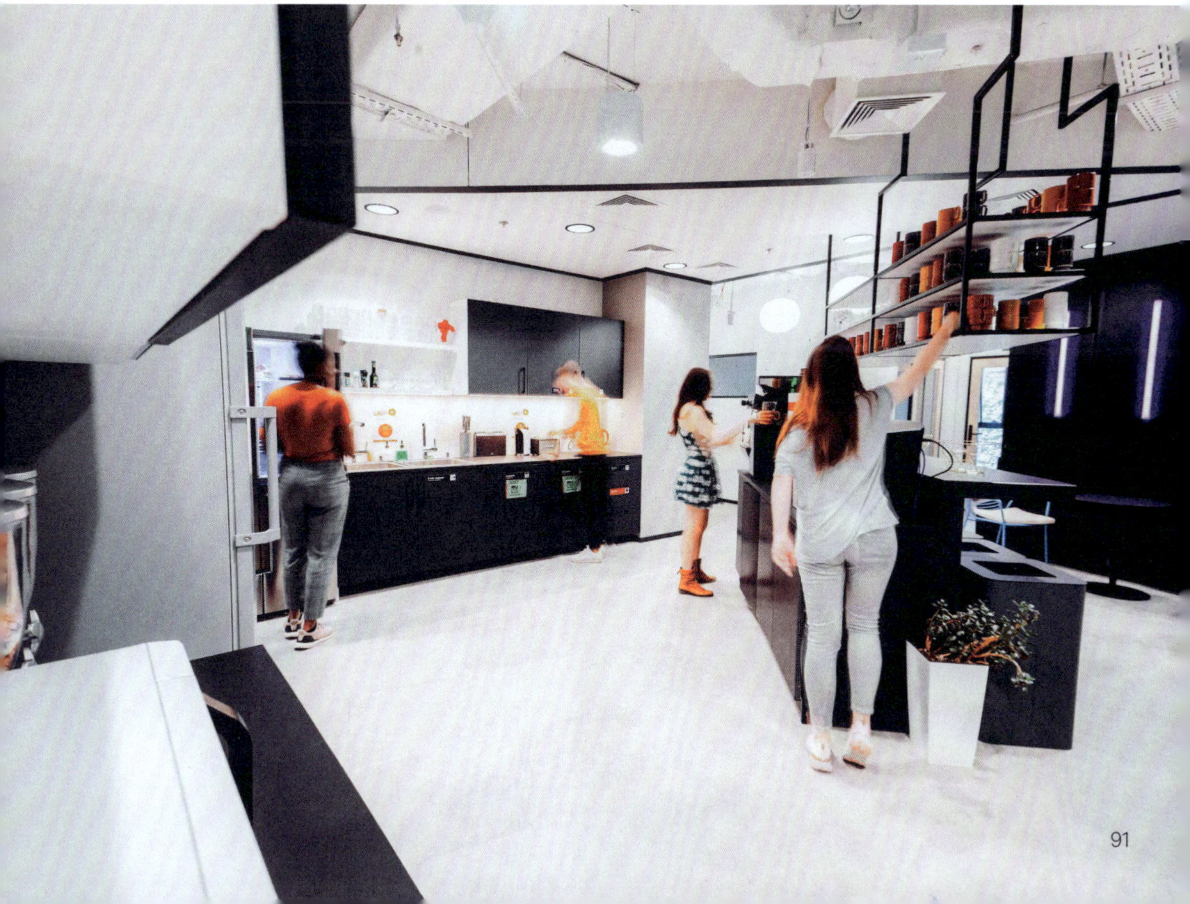

Face of the Space:

Jerzy Brodzikowski, the general manager of CIC Warsaw, is one of the friendly faces behind the space. He has extensive experience across the coworking and serviced-office sector in Poland, having worked in the industry for many years. He is passionate about meeting new people and acting as a connector and conductor to help the startup ecosystem at CIC Warsaw and beyond to thrive and grow.

[Name] # District Hall

[Address] Varso Place, ul. Chmielna 73, 00-801 Warsaw

[Total Area]

700m²

[Workspaces]

150

[The Story] District Hall, which opened in July 2020, was inspired by Tim Rowe's approach to coworking spaces as innovation centers where money, talents and ideas come together. Tim is not only the founder of Cambridge Innovation Center, one of the first and largest coworking spaces in the US, but also the founder of Venture Café, a nonprofit organization which aims to develop the local innovation ecosystem. One of Venture Café's projects in Poland is District Hall, a public innovation space in the heart of Warsaw and one of the first free coworking spaces in the city.

District Hall's lounge is a free workspace that brings together early-stage entrepreneurs, expats and startups. It provides members with unlimited access to high-speed internet, a café and a podcast studio. The space also offers event halls and conference rooms, and it organizes workshops and the Thursday Gathering Weekly Meetup, which brings users of the space together and encourages collaborations between innovators. It was able to remain open throughout the pandemic, which was helpful for many people who did not have access to an office space at home.

[Links] **Web:** venturecafewarsaw.org **LinkedIn:** company/venturecafewarsaw
Facebook: venturecafewarsaw **Instagram:** @venturecafe_warsaw

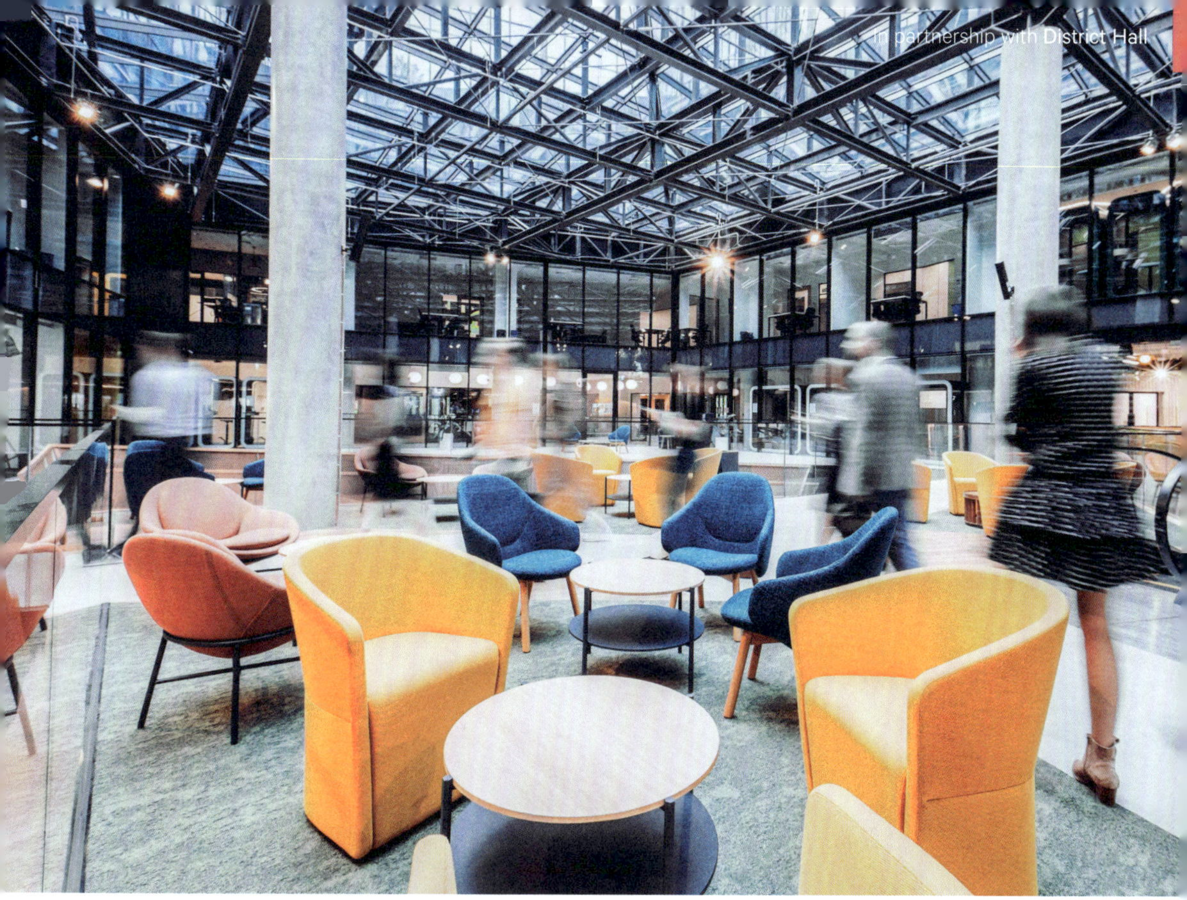

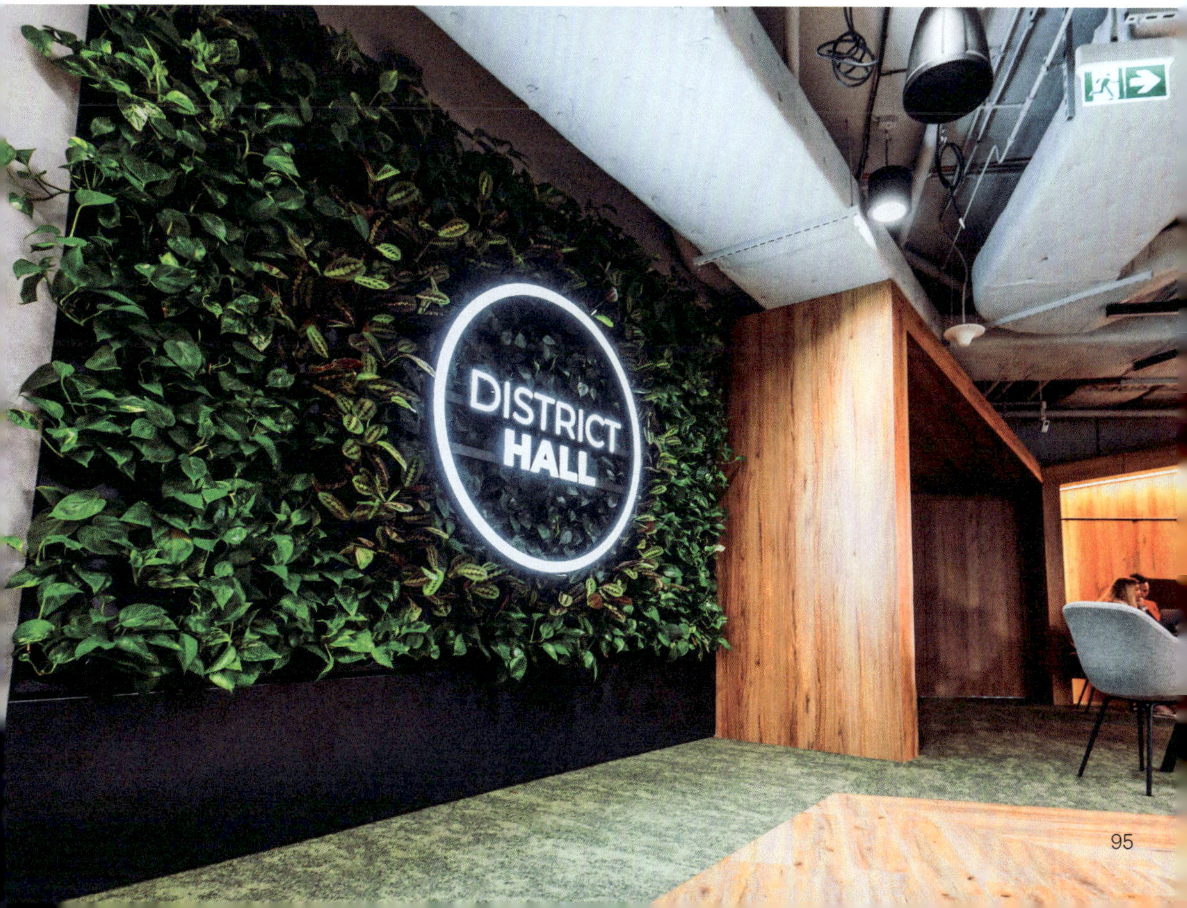
DISTRICT
HALL

Face of the Space:

Ewa Geresz, the director of programs and global partnerships at Venture Café Warsaw, is responsible for several programs that strengthen the innovation environment in Poland and connect it globally. Ewa's previous experience includes working on international projects and serving as the president of SIETAR Poland.

Aureliusz Górski is an innovation ecosystem facilitator who is on a lifelong mission to support the transformation of the startup landscape across Poland. Aureliusz is also a cofounder of CIC Warsaw, an innovation center, and the founding executive director at Venture Café Warsaw Foundation.

[Name] # Google for Startups Campus Warsaw

[Address] Centrum Praskie Koneser ul, Plac Konesera 10, 03-736 Warsaw

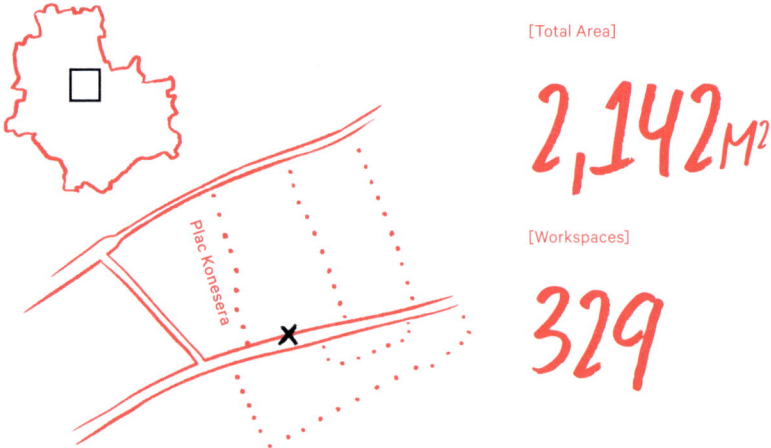

[Total Area]

2,142m²

[Workspaces]

329

[The Story] In November 2015, Google for Startups Campus opened its doors for entrepreneurs from Poland and across the CEE region. Ever since, Google for Startups Campus has become a home for programs, events and a growing community of startup founders. Its mission is to connect startups with the right people, products and best practices to help them grow and create a community of like-minded people. The Google for Startups Campus community brings together founders and employees of startups as well as investors and organizations supporting the development of young companies.

In total, almost 100,000 people have visited the Google for Startups Campus Warsaw location since it opened in 2015. By March 2020, it had organized 1,500 events in its space, averaging three hours of events a day. Google's support goes far beyond the walls of the space. Google for Startups in Warsaw helps startups at various stages of growth, from different backgrounds and across borders. These startups create a community of over 7,500 members developing 1,800 startups, including 1,200 Polish startups (26 percent of Poland's startup ecosystem) and 600 CEE startups.

[Links] Web: campus.co/warsaw LinkedIn: showcase/google-for-startups
Facebook: GoogleForStartups Instagram: @googleforstartups Twitter: @GoogleStartups

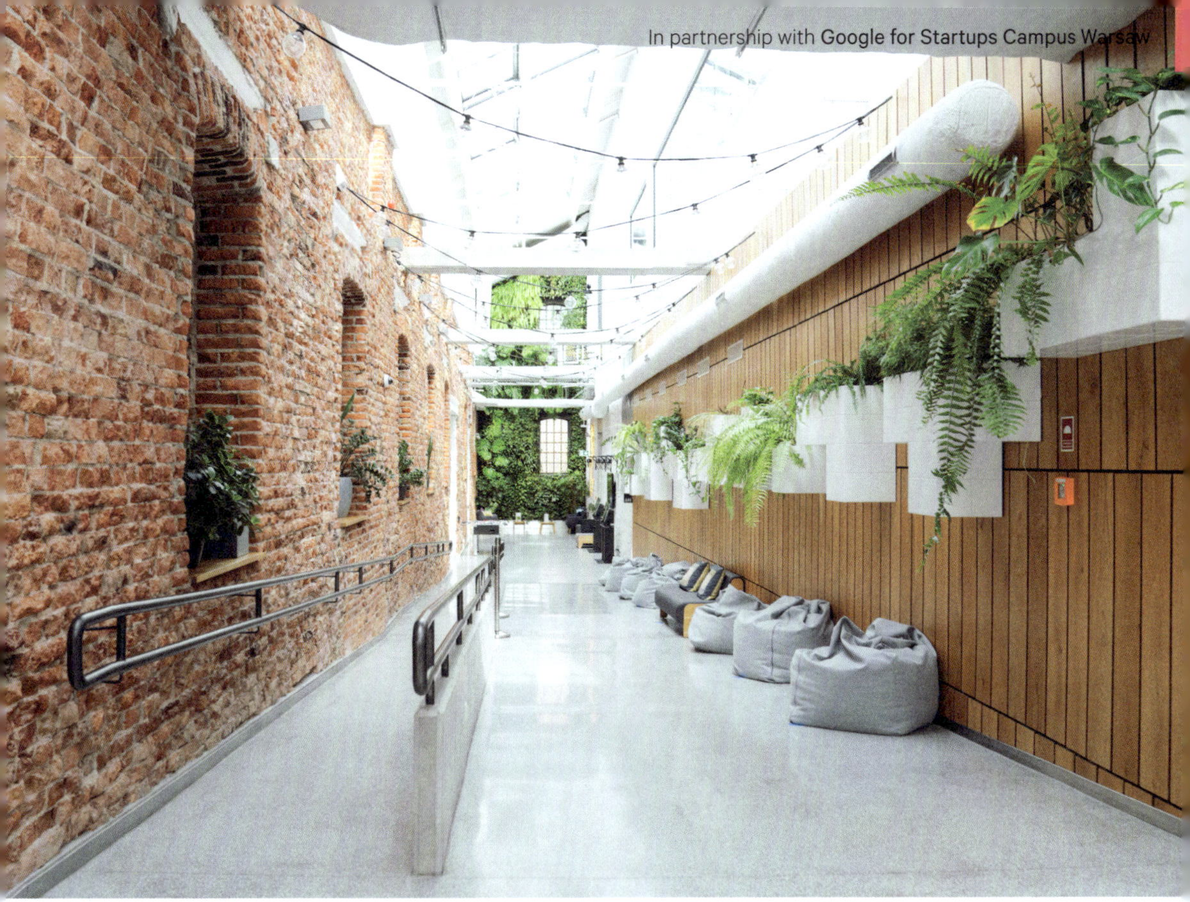

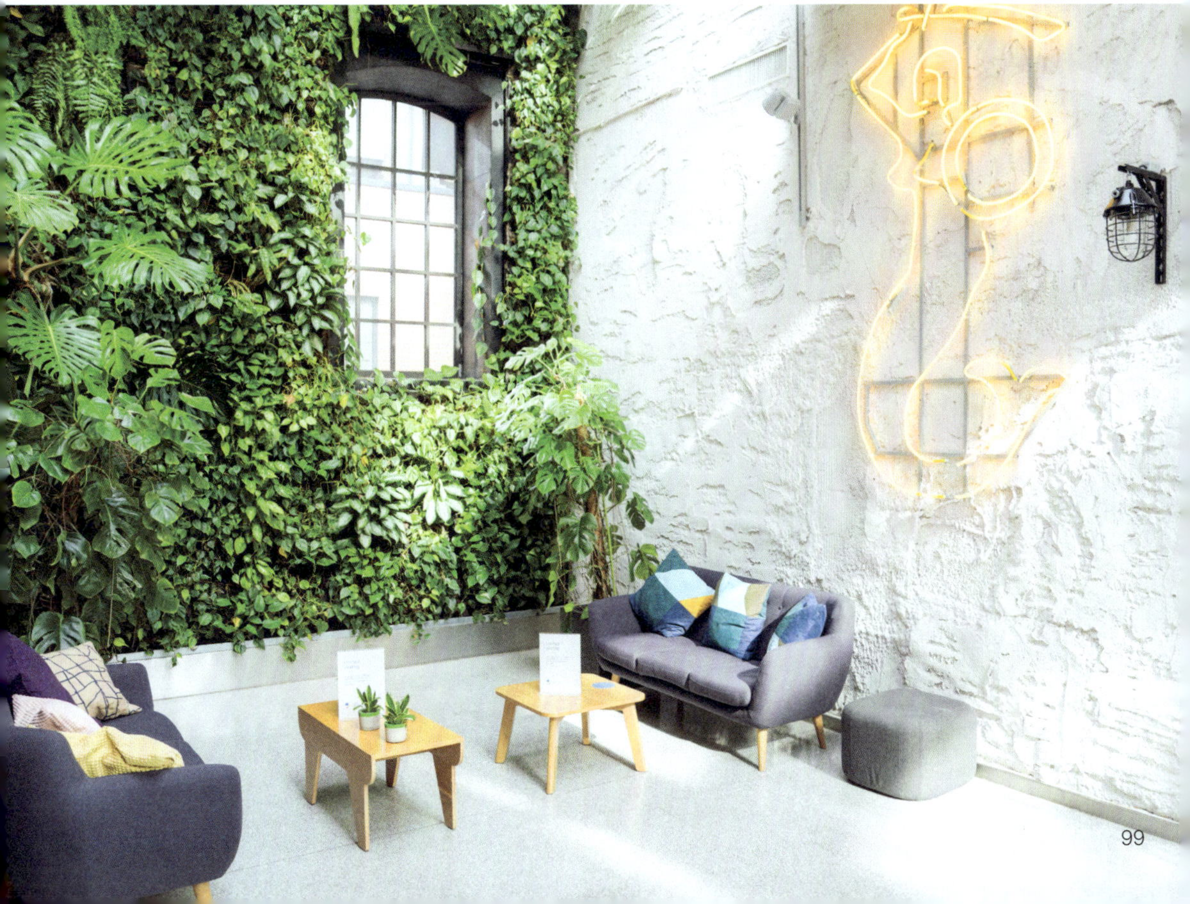

Face of the Space:

Michał Kramarz has been in the Internet industry since 2004. He joined Google in 2006 as one of the first employees in Poland, responsible for development of Google's collaboration with retail, ecommerce, finance and travel industries. In October 2019, he became the head of Google for Startups in Central Europe, leading the Campus in Warsaw. Michał has also supported many Polish startups in expanding their business outside the country.

[Name] # HubHub

[Address] Nowogrodzka Square, al. Jerozolimskie 93, 02-001 Warsaw

[Total Area]

2,744M²

[Workspaces]

375

[The Story] HubHub was created in 2017 by European property developer HB Reavis to form a coworking environment that supports and encourages startups to grow into established businesses. It has grown to have locations in five European countries. Its Warsaw space is in the city center, across from HB Reavis' Varso Tower on Nowogrodzka Square. Freelancers and startup teams can choose from fixed or flexible desks, private offices or several offices for a growing team. All members have access to twenty-one private rooms for calls or meetings. HubHub also hosts networking events, demo days and competitions with partners (such as Reactor X and Huge Thing) and HubHub members (such as MIT Enterprise Forum CEE and Youth Business Poland) in its modern event space.

Leveraging its international locations, HubHub runs cross-regional initiatives such as the Future Now conference, where one competition prize is membership at HubHub. This was how Renderro, a cloud-based desktop for content creators' resource-heavy tasks, started working at the Nowogrodzka Square space. The Renderro team report that HubHub gathers proactive and creative people, which adds to the atmosphere, improving their well being and motivation to work.

[Links] Web: hubhub.com/en/warsaw-nowogrodzka-square LinkedIn: company/hub-hub
Facebook: hubhubcowork Instagram: @hubhub_cowork Twitter: @hubhubcowork

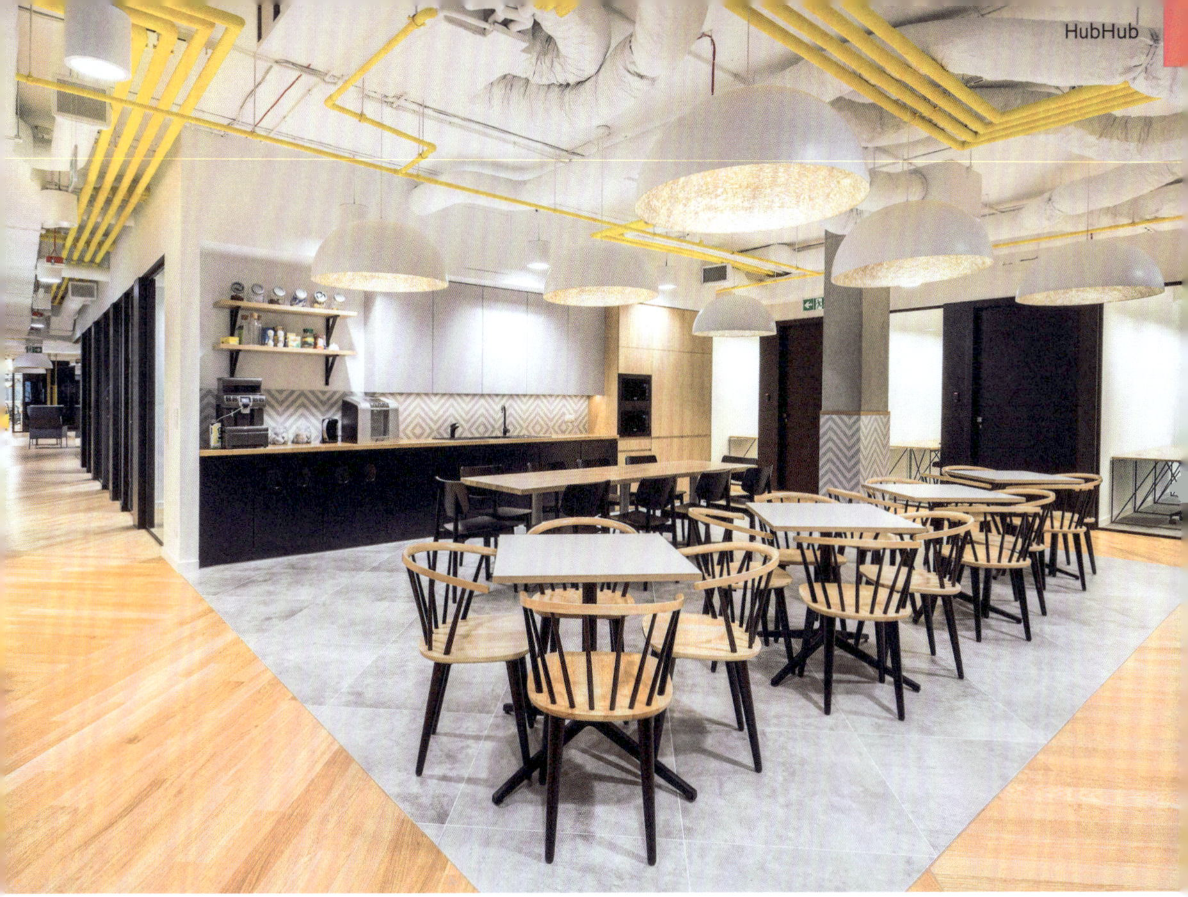

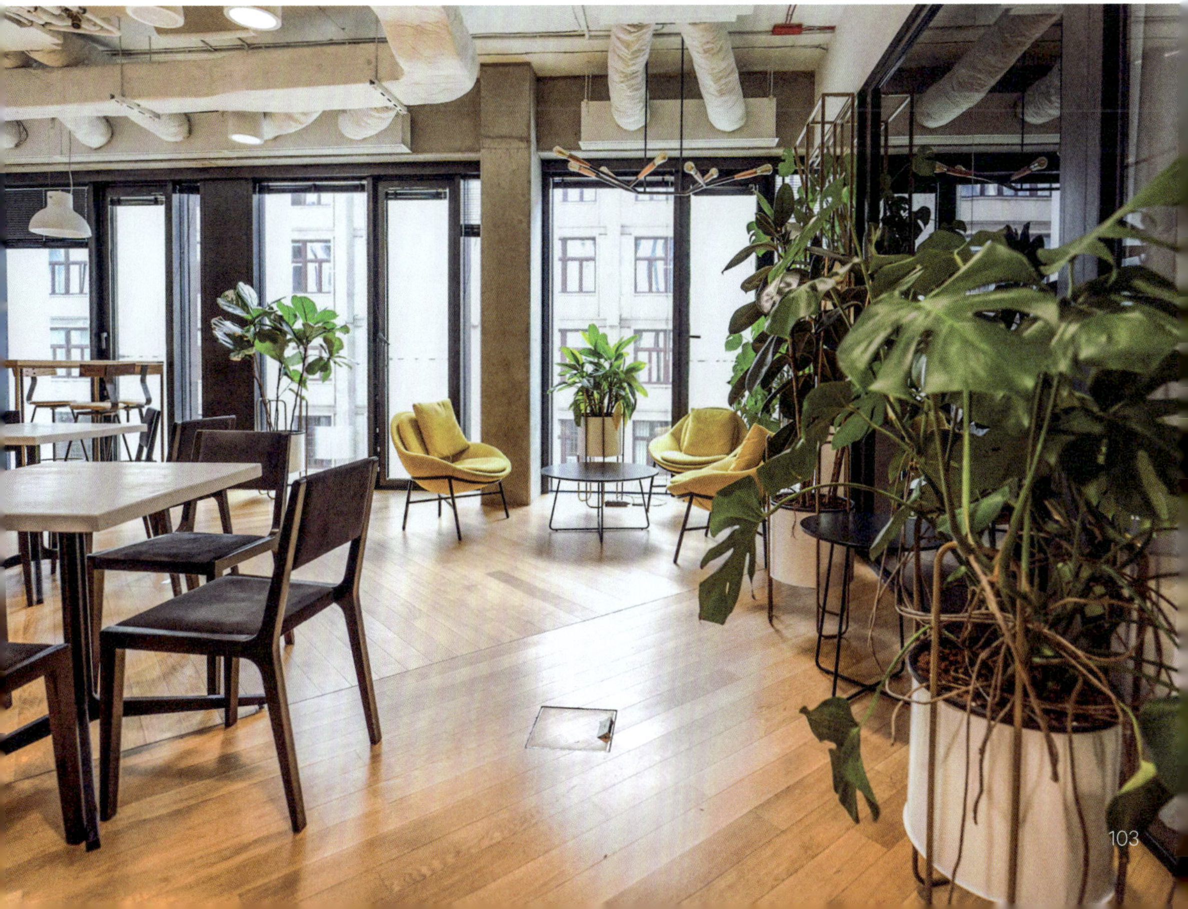

Face of the Space:

Agata Roszko is a community manager at HubHub Nowogrodzka, where she is responsible for taking the community relations to a higher level with both HubHub members and partners.
She began her work in the startup ecosystem in 2017, helping entrepreneurs launch their ideas in the Polish market, and she continues to support them by creating a thriving community at HubHub.

[Name] # Mindspace Koszyki

[Address] ul. Koszykowa 61 and 65, 00-667 Warsaw

[Total Area]

5,500M²

[Workspaces]

780

Koszykowa

[The Story] Launched in Israel in 2014, Mindspace is a global flex-office provider with thirty-two locations across Europe, the US and Israel. Mindspace redefines and reimagines workspaces by placing community at their heart, offering highly personalized customer service and beautiful places to work. Great care and attention is paid to the look and feel of every location, and interiors and artworks are sourced from local artisans and makers. Building a community and providing exemplary service that is adaptive and accommodating to the ever-changing needs of how people work is of great importance to the company.

Mindspace Koszyki opened in 2017 and was one of the first providers of flex-office spaces in Warsaw. Ideally located in the center of the city, next to the cosmopolitan and historic Hala Koszyki food hall, Mindspace Koszyki has excellent access to public transport. Its flexible membership options offer both small and large businesses affordable, design-led space on monthly or longer term contracts. With sumptuous interiors, fully equipped kitchens, meeting rooms, an onsite barista service, all-inclusive amenities and exclusive events, Mindspace Koszyki offers members a warm and welcoming place to work. All members also have access to an app which offers an array of discounts and benefits from local partners, and members can work from any Mindspace location worldwide at no additional cost.

[Links] Web: **mindspace.me/warsaw** LinkedIn: **showcase/mindspace-warsaw** Facebook: **mindspace.me** Instagram: **@mindspace.me** Twitter: **@MindspaceME**

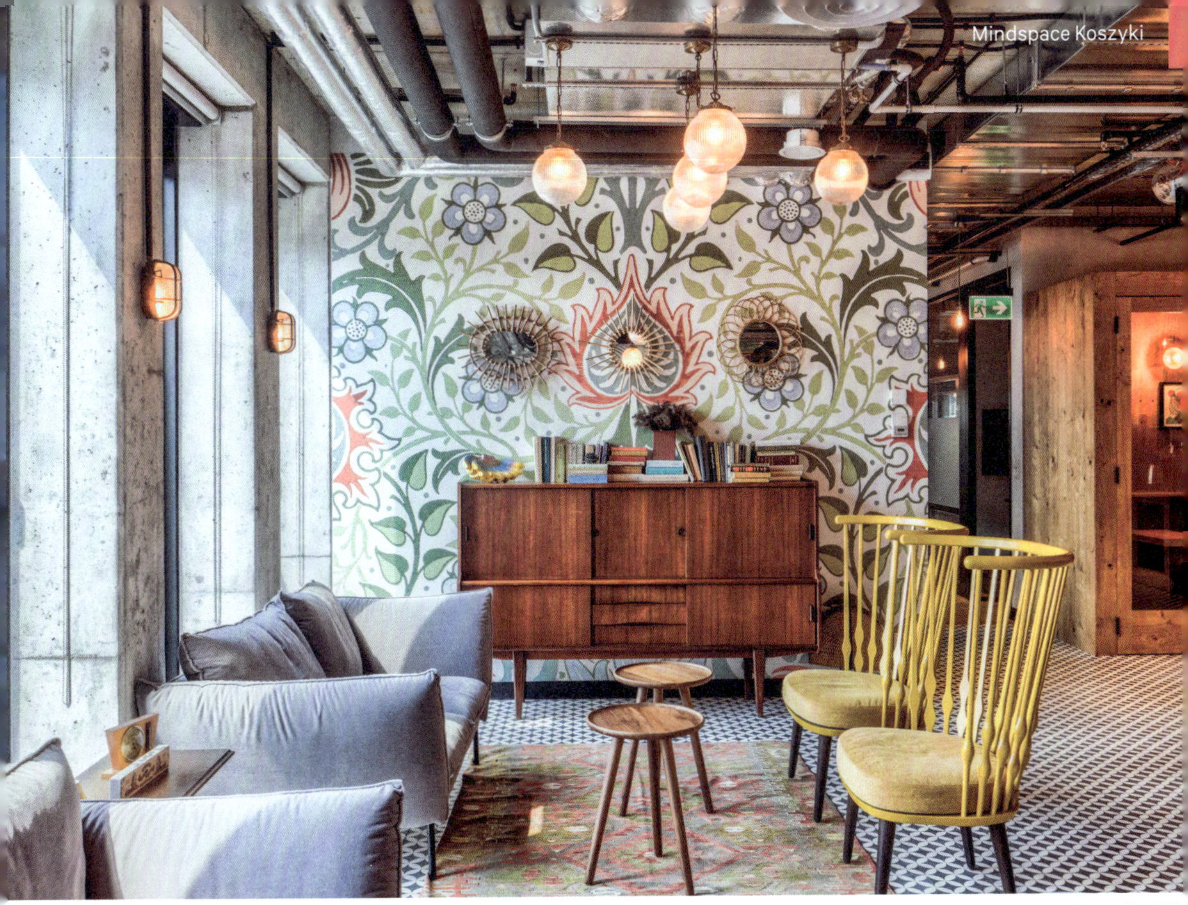

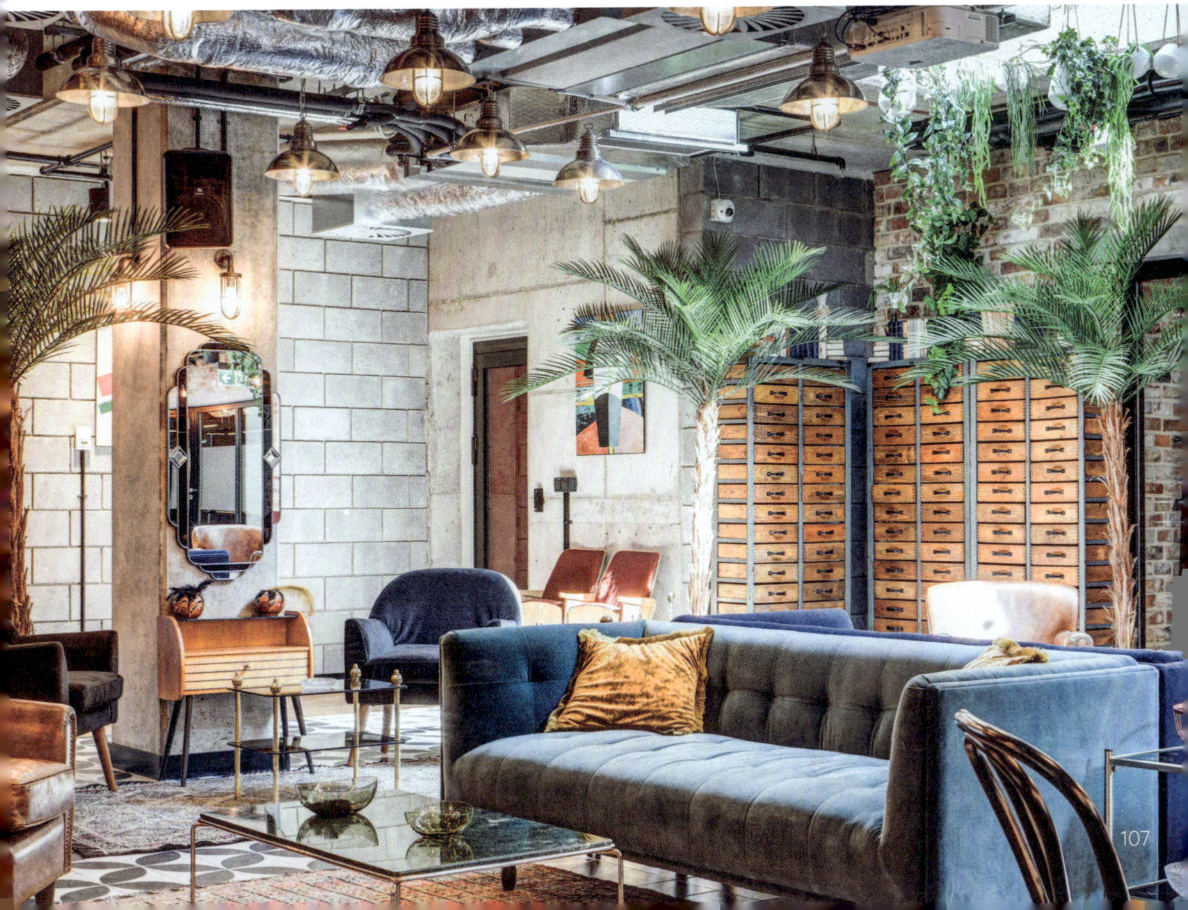

Face of the Space:

As the city lead for Mindspace in Poland, Michał Kwinta brings a wealth of experience from the tourism and hospitality industry, having worked for many travel companies. He has been with Mindspace since the inception of its Polish branch in 2017, and he is now responsible for Mindspace's operations, development and expansion in Warsaw. He loves to work with people, help solve their problems and provide exceptional customer service.

[Name] # WeWork

[Address] Grzybowska 60, 00-844 Warsaw

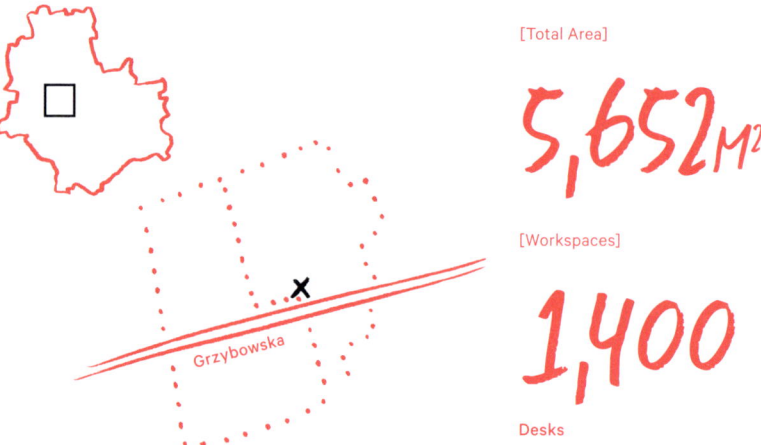

[Total Area]

5,652M²

[Workspaces]

1,400

Desks

[The Story] WeWork Grzybowska 60 opened in July 2020, as the fifth building of WeWork in Warsaw. Members of the WeWork community can enjoy the view of the Wola district from the ninth-floor terrace as well as having full access to the space's sister WeWork location, Grzybowska 62. The two spaces operate together as a single location, which allows the members to move freely between buildings and access all common areas, conference rooms and other amenities, including secure bicycle parking inside and outside the building, showers and changing rooms.

The space offers hot desks, dedicated desks and private offices, which allows for the support of small businesses and enterprise companies alike. Enterprise companies, currently making up 51 percent of WeWork memberships, can take advantage of WeWork's enterprise offering, which includes a range of options, from a private custom floor to serve as a corporate headquarters to private flexible satellite offices for corporations to house local sales, marketing, engineering or innovation teams. Since September 2021, the Grzybowska 60 building has been part of Growth Campus Europe, an initiative launched by WeWork to boost economic recovery across nine European countries, including Poland.

[Links] Web: wework.com/l/office-space/warsaw LinkedIn: company/wework Facebook: wework Instagram: @wework Twitter: @wework

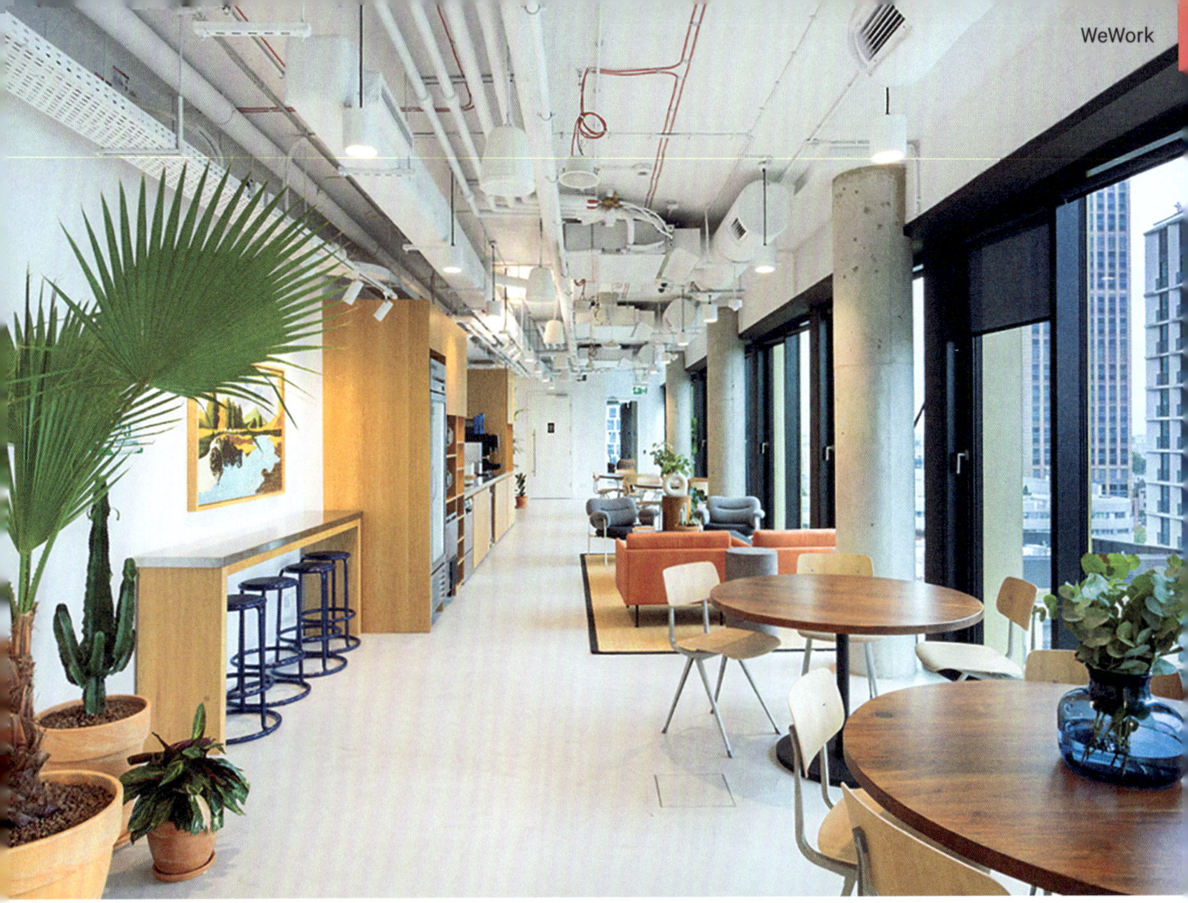

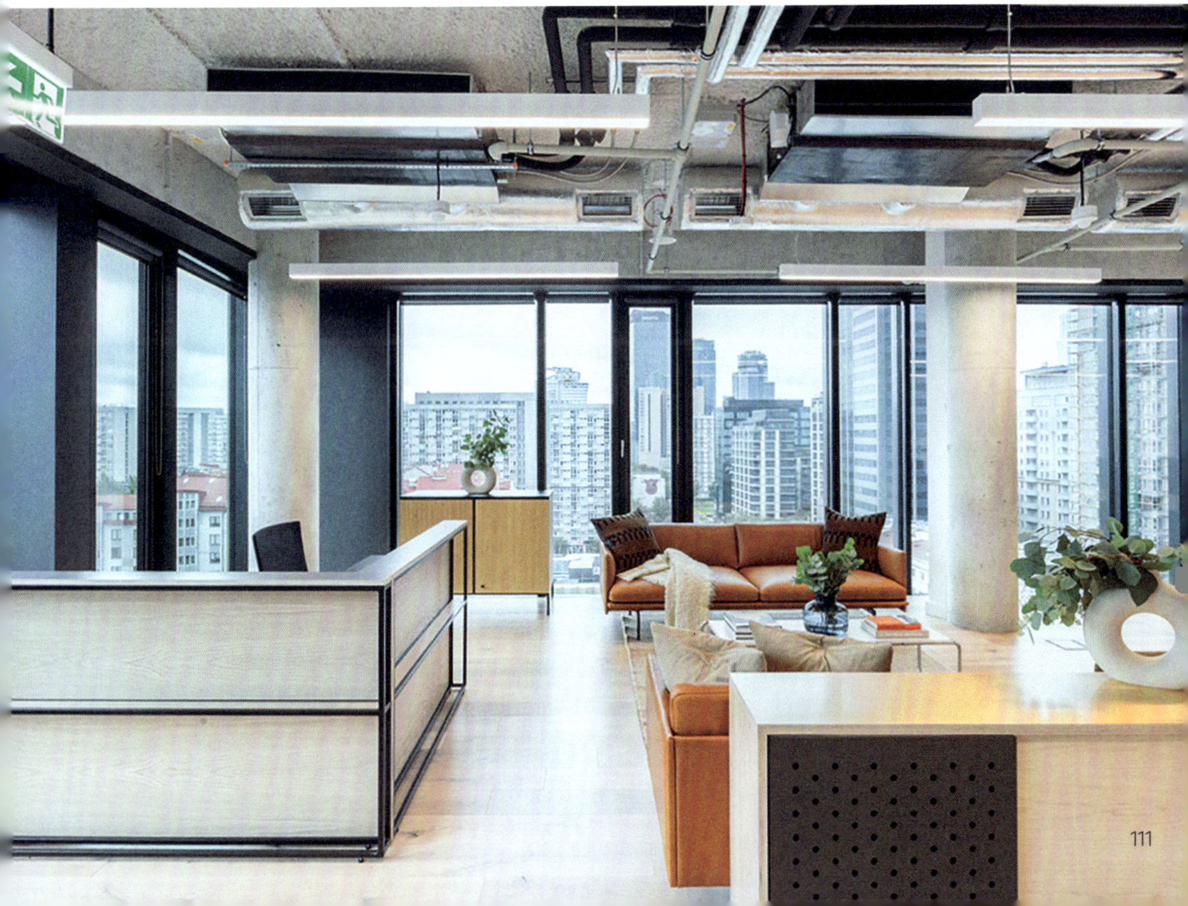

Face of the Space:

Marta Kurowicka is the community manager of WeWork Grzybowska Street 60 and 62. Born and raised in Warsaw, she relocated to London in 2003.
In 2018, she returned to Warsaw with a degree in business administration from Kingston University and began her work at WeWork. Marta is a front-line contact for all customers located in her buildings and is responsible for building strong communities among a broad range of companies from many industries.

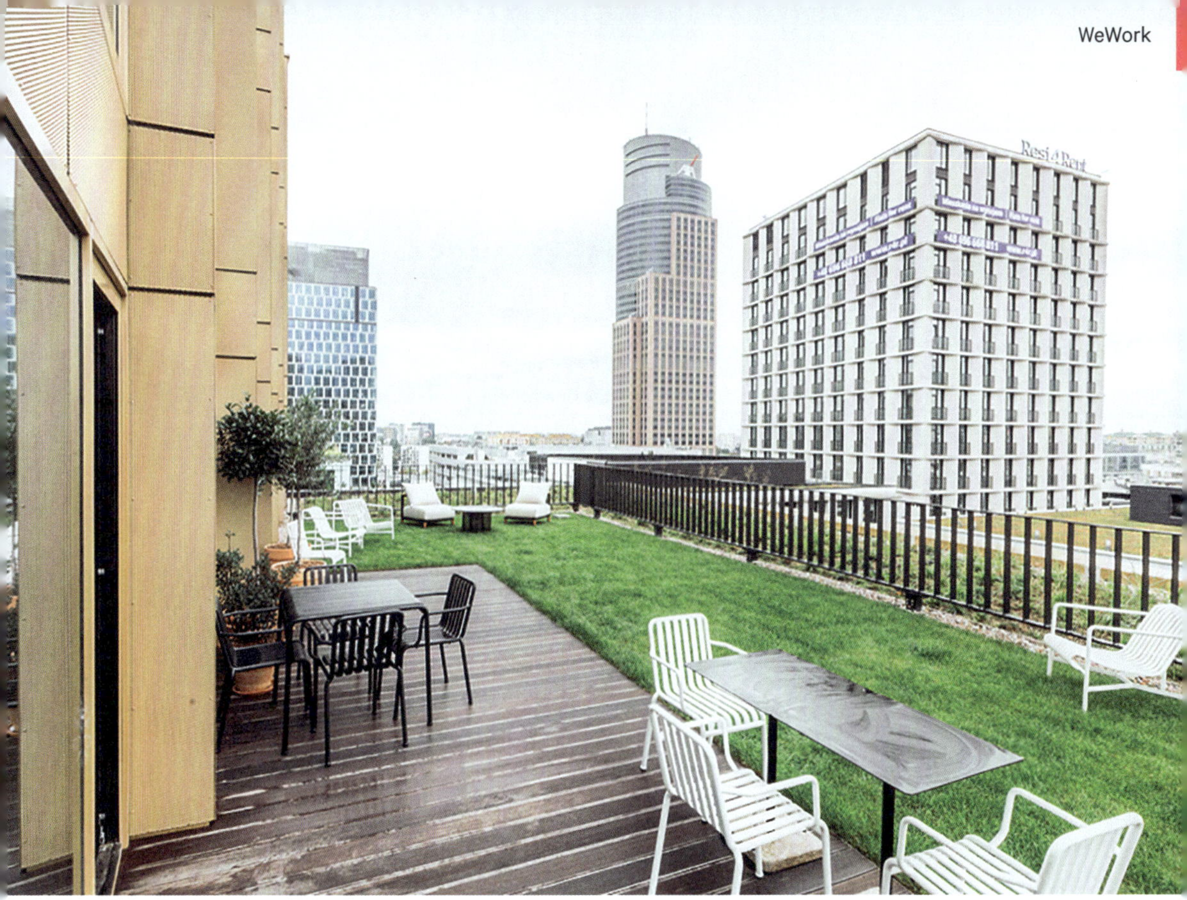

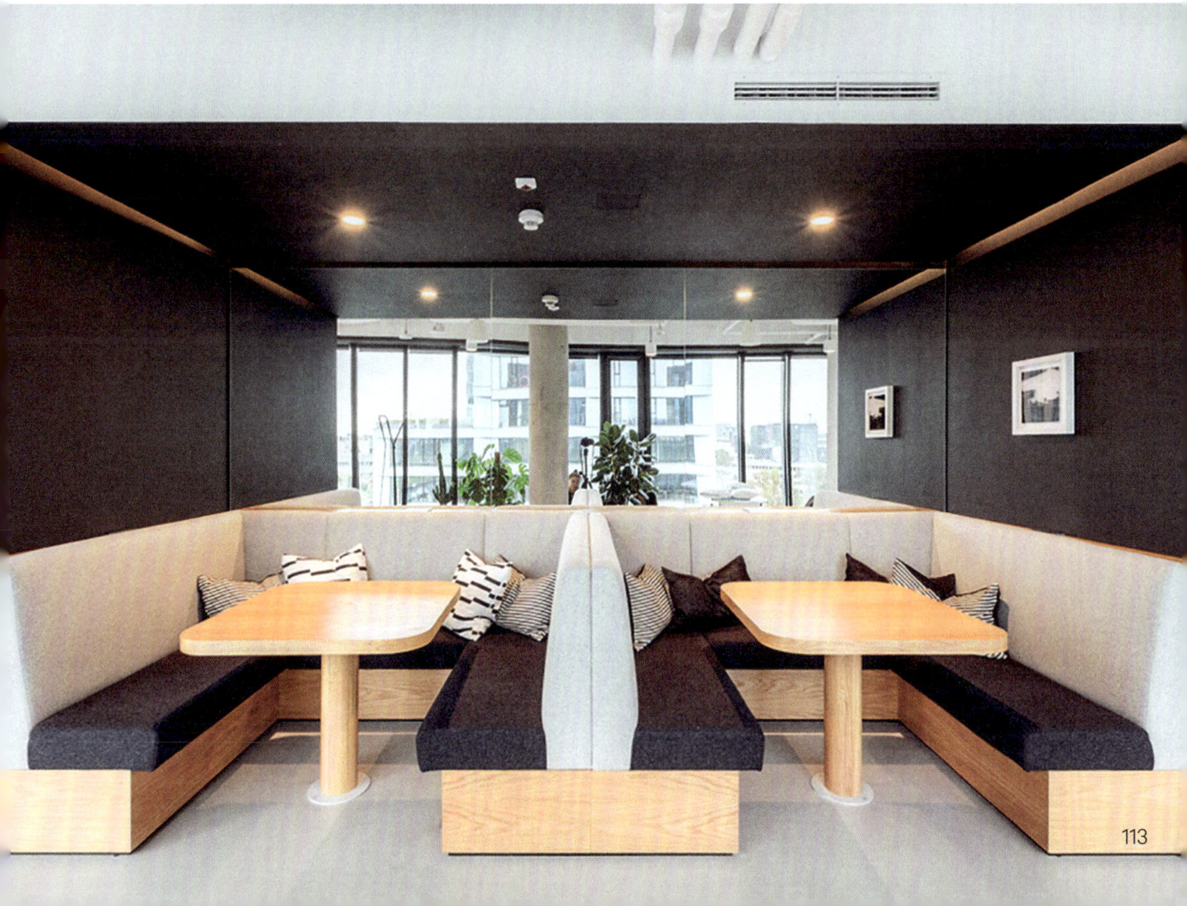

erts

In partnership with:

INNO
VATE
OR
DIE

A Guiding Light for Energy Startups

Jakub Miler / CEO, EIT InnoEnergy Central Europe

[Sector]   **Energy**

Jakub Miler knows all about the challenges of complex markets. Before joining EIT InnoEnergy in 2014, he held international leadership positions in the engineering sector, including in the mining, construction and energy industries. At EIT InnoEnergy, he works with academic, industrial and financial sectors to accelerate breakthrough cleantech innovations and help startups get to market in a complex, dynamic and highly regulated field.

In contrast to other sectors, energy-solution development can take three to four years, particularly for CAPEX-heavy hardware, so founders need extra reserves of patience and perseverance. The biggest obstacle is regulation. The European Commission is working to unify this across the continent, but it still varies widely and regularly lags behind innovation. One example is waste-to-energy solutions, which face strict restrictions on what materials can be used. Having developed a zero-emissions solution using sawdust from Ikea, Swedish energy company Meva Energy thought they'd finally cracked the market. Convincing the regulator, however, took many more years. "In these cases," says Jakub, "you need very patient, specialized investors with big pockets. The company has now closed contracts for forty million euros and will potentially float on the stock market, but until last year they didn't know if they'd make it."

Supported by the European Institute of Innovation and Technology (EIT), which is a body of the European Union, EIT InnoEnergy bridges the gap between industry, innovation, politics and academia and is country- and tech-agnostic. This means it has access to the most exciting developments, is well placed to understand cross-sectoral challenges, and helps to shape the future. "We're ahead of the curve compared to everyone else," says Jakub. "We monitor and support emerging technologies and the regulations that will shape the market in five to ten years."

EIT InnoEnergy also advises startups on EU funding opportunities. It connects them with the industry suppliers and OEMs (original equipment manufacturers) they need to create strategic global value chains for the manufacture and distribution of highly complex products such as batteries and other hardware.

Somewhere between an accelerator and a VC fund – but much more than either – EIT InnoEnergy is both an investor and investment advisor. It helps startups boost their appeal by, among other things, landing that first contract that proves commercial viability.

Most important tips for startups:

- **Look for specialized investors who are sympathetic to your challenges.** Developing cleantech takes years and costs billions, and innovation normally outstrips legislation, so you need patient investors with big pockets.

- **Create strategic value chains.** Cleantech solutions have long, complex production processes and supply chains. There's no way you can go at it alone.

- **Think collaboration, not competition.** Energy is such a wide-open, fast-growing market that there's room for everyone and all players stand to gain from innovations.

- **Aim for disruptive business models as well as disruptive tech.** The energy sector has no universally recognizable brands that command customer loyalty and can shape trends. If your solution helps democratize energy consumption, you're onto a winner.

"It's not a classic accelerator or an orthodox approach," says Jakub. "It's more 'What's needed, what can we do, and who can we connect you with?' The focus isn't on the technology or stage of development but the impact, the CO_2 reduction. The bigger it is, the more interested we are."

InnoEnergy also runs its own master's programs to equip the brightest and best technical and engineering graduates to succeed in a changing world. It has a strong focus on entrepreneurship. "We're not really trying to shape people becoming part of the corporate world but actually building their companies."

Among other competencies, EIT InnoEnergy advises entrepreneurs on how to take advantage of the opportunities offered by current industry transformation. "Regulations may differ," says Jakub, "but everyone is working towards a common target, which is a decarbonized Europe by 2050. Anything contributing to that key objective can expect a lot of support."

The holy grail now, he says, is the reliable generation and storage of renewable energy, and InnoEnergy is currently investing heavily in tech like photovoltaic cells and hydrogen generation (for chemical energy storage). "If you come up with something that makes hardware cheaper and easier to produce, less reliant on very scarce natural materials, or makes hydrogen generation cheaper, it's going to be a hit."

From the business-model perspective, companies that contribute to the democratization of energy production and accelerate solution adoption are also highly sought after. "The energy system is a bit behind, say, the banking sector or the communications sector, where you can get a pay-as-you-go phone for one euro," says Jakub. "We can't just create breakthrough technologies by improving only the specs. You can only have an impact when the price or value proposition is attractive and customers are willing to buy." He's confident this is around the corner, though. "We're in a sweet spot now where awareness is so high that consumer behavior will drive the big companies to change."

About

EIT InnoEnergy is the largest sustainable energy-innovation ecosystem in the world and part of a pan-European knowledge innovation community spanning industry, academia and the third sector. It invests €100 million ($120 million) annually in innovative cleantech products and services like battery storage, green hydrogen and solar photovoltaics that reduce energy costs and greenhouse gas emissions and boost system performance, job creation and industry competitiveness. For startups and scaleups, it provides investment, connections and tailored support to de-risk disruptive innovations and accelerate time to market.

[Contact]   Email: ce@innoenergy.com Telephone: +48124467040

[Links]   Web: innoenergy.com LinkedIn: company/innoenergy
Facebook: innoenergyEU Twitter: @InnoEnergyEU

" *We can't just create breakthrough technologies by improving only the specs. You can only have an impact when the price or value proposition is attractive and customers are willing to buy.* "

Broadening the Horizons of High-Tech Startups

Michał Kramarz / Head of Google for Startups, Central Europe

[Sector]   Information technology

With over fifteen years' experience developing export, entrepreneurship and commercial sectors at Google, Michał Kramarz knows exactly what it takes to succeed internationally. As head of the tech company's startup initiatives in Central Europe, it's his responsibility to make sure alumni are equipped with everything they need to go out and conquer the world.

Poland is one of the most dynamic startup ecosystems in the CEE region. Compared to other European hubs, it's particularly rich in high-tech startups. This is thanks to a combination of high-quality education and competitive salaries, which make it a great place to hire top talent. "B2B SaaS is in this region's blood," says Michał. He believes this is down to, ironically, a historical lack of investment: B2C tech solutions tend to require significant upfront investment to drive large-scale user acquisition. B2B business models, however, can often scale more slowly with fewer resources once they manage to secure their first few corporate customers.

With over half a billion dollars invested in startups in 2020, Poland is rapidly catching up to other countries and attracting growing interest from overseas. Now, says Michał, Polish startups need to step up and take their place on the international stage. "Here, the size of the market is both an opportunity and a threat. It's one of the bigger markets in Europe, but medium-sized compared to the rest of the world. So if you want to go big, you need to look outside of Poland." The CEE region is also home to a wide range of verticals, with gamedev, healthtech, ecommerce and edutech all current hotbeds of activity. "All the things the pandemic accelerated, basically. So, you can find every kind of startup and tech here, but there's space for more. At the same time, the size of each specific market is relatively small, so you need to think big to grow the business. This means building on an international scale from the beginning."

To help startups do this, Google assigns specialized in-house and industry experts as mentors in its Google for Startups Accelerator program. They are there to address the specific issues faced by each fledgling company. The whole C-level team is encouraged to participate: CTOs can learn the latest technologies and polish their product, CMOs can gain knowledge on analytics and user acquisition, while CEOs learn from Google leadership and its unique culture. "The idea is that when they connect all the elements, they have the full set of competencies they need to grow."

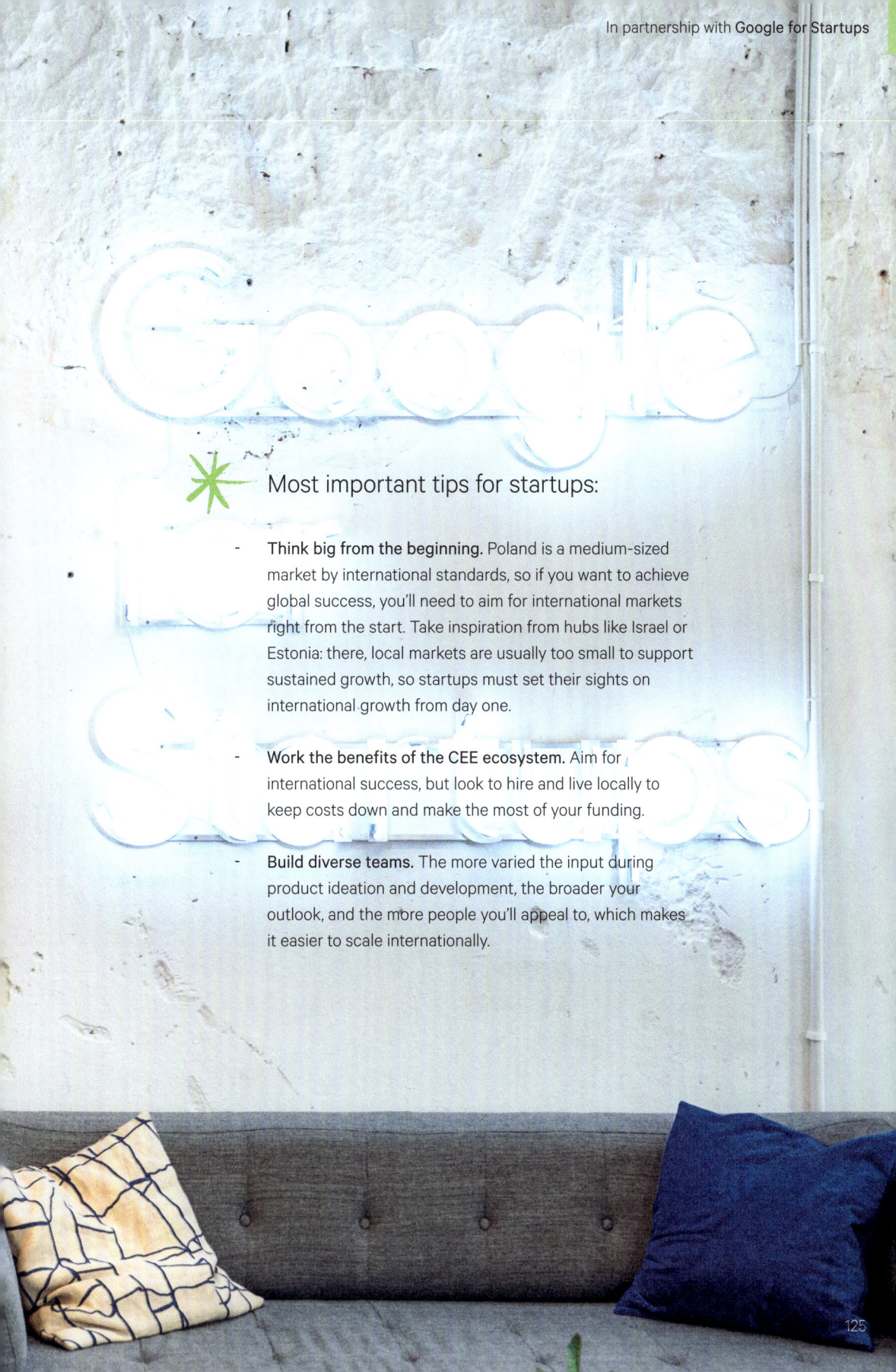

Most important tips for startups:

- **Think big from the beginning.** Poland is a medium-sized market by international standards, so if you want to achieve global success, you'll need to aim for international markets right from the start. Take inspiration from hubs like Israel or Estonia: there, local markets are usually too small to support sustained growth, so startups must set their sights on international growth from day one.

- **Work the benefits of the CEE ecosystem.** Aim for international success, but look to hire and live locally to keep costs down and make the most of your funding.

- **Build diverse teams.** The more varied the input during product ideation and development, the broader your outlook, and the more people you'll appeal to, which makes it easier to scale internationally.

Michał believes diversity of viewpoints is also important for successful product development. "The more diverse your teams are, the better your products will be and the more people they'll appeal to." Unfortunately, however, diversity isn't something the tech world is known for. So, to address the yawning ethnic and gender gap, Google also runs dedicated programs for Black and women founders. "Google for Startups' mission is to level the playing field for founders in different industries, so they can operate from Warsaw or elsewhere in the region as they would in Silicon Valley or other places: by getting access to people, technology and funding."

More varied viewpoints can also help tech founders corner new markets. While the region has birthed success stories such as DocPlanner, Booksy and CD Projekt Red, Michał believes it could achieve even more if STEAM graduates were able to put perfectionism aside now and again. "In mathematics and physics, for example, you need to be exact about what you're building – detailed. People are taught this way for years, and when they build solutions, they try to do it that way too. So the quality is always high, but the speed could be faster, even if that meant sometimes sacrificing a bit of the initial quality."

Despite this, however, Michał believes the CEE region is a great place to be right now. "More and more investment funds are showing interest. So, entrepreneurs should think internationally and attract international investment but operate from here, because the ecosystem is developing very fast."

About

Google for Startups Campus in Warsaw is part of a global network of top tech hubs, accelerators and diversity-oriented organizations across 125 countries. It delivers hands-on and virtual training, resources and programs for entrepreneurs in a range of industries, including tailored support for Black and women founders. Now in its sixth year, Campus in Warsaw connects 1,800 startups in its community with the best of Google tech, know-how, leadership and best practices to prepare them to attract investment and conquer global markets.

[Contact]   Email: campus.co/warsaw

[Links]   Web: campus.co/warsaw LinkedIn: showcase/google-for-startups
Facebook: GoogleForStartups Instagram: @googleforstartups
Twitter: @GoogleStartups

"The more diverse your teams are, the better your products will be and the more people they'll appeal to."

Fast-Forwarding Fintech in Central and Eastern Europe

Dawid Galus / Manager, Digital Innovation

[Sector]   **Finance**

With fifteen years' experience in the financial sector, Dawid Galus is well placed to understand the challenges faced by fintech startups. As manager of Santander Bank Polska's Digital Innovation Office, he's responsible for coordinating collaborations with startups as well as representing the bank in the AccelUP Acceleration Program. He's also accredited by the Polish Bank Association to evaluate fintech applications for EU subsidies.

With some 270 startups, Poland is the largest fintech hub in CEE, and the sector is an important driver of the economy. In 2020 alone, the country saw a rise of almost seventy percent in VC funding across the board, with over $50 million going to fintechs.

Unlike in some ecosystems that experience fierce competition between startups and incumbents, in Poland the established financial institutions play a key role in developing the sector. "It simply wouldn't be possible without a well-developed system of financing as part of acceleration programs that promote cooperation with mature financial institutions," says Dawid. "From the technological perspective, fintech startups are well prepared to offer their products on the market, but many struggle to navigate market realities, so they need support with pricing models and valuation of their solution when negotiating with potential customers."

Collaboration with a mature corporate partner can also slash time to market and smooth the way when developing solutions for certain challenges specific to the financial services and products market. In the case of crowdfunding platforms, for example, the involvement of an institution like Santander Brokerage Poland helps startups to comply with the requirements of the Polish Financial Supervision Authority (PFSA), without which they wouldn't be able to operate.

In other areas, legal, technological and market conditions simply make it difficult for startups to compete with established institutions, so it's important to be aware of this. For example, when it comes to deferred payment services, fintechs dominate.

By contrast, incumbents hold sway over loans and credits, making it much harder to disrupt the market. "Before launching a product," says Dawid, "it's vital for startups to analyze the area they intend to operate in and judge whether they can compete against established financial institutions or whether the best approach would be to seek a partnership."

Chopin

Pokój
spotkań

Santander
Centrum Relacyjne

Most important tips for startups:

- **Research your target market well.** Finance is a complex and highly regulated sector. Before developing a product or service, you need to know whether you can compete with the incumbents or whether you'd be better off partnering with them.

- **See incumbents as potential partners and customers rather than the competition.** That way, everyone stands to win.

- **Take advantage of corporate collaborations to test your solution.** There's no better test environment than a mature institution that's representative of your target customer base. Plus, securing an incumbent as your first customer helps to establish market confidence in your solution.

- **Seek support to validate your product and establish its market value.** It'll put you in a stronger position when negotiating with potential customers.

Establishing this kind of commercial collaboration with fintechs is central to Santander's modus operandi, and the bank has created a tailor-made process for startups undergoing legal and technology review to help them achieve compliance. It also provides infrastructure to test and refine IT architecture and determine whether solutions can be integrated into the bank's systems. This valuable experience stands startups in good stead when they go on to collaborate with other companies.

At the proof-of-concept stage, the bank works closely with fintechs to ensure MVPs are as close to the final product as possible, which helps accelerate commercial implementation and joint revenue generation. There are no hard-and-fast requirements for collaboration, but ideally the bank seeks startups that have a product or service at the late MVP stage and paying customers.

As well as benefiting from test environments and support, startups working with AI and machine learning in particular get valuable access to anonymized documents to train algorithms that can have cross-sectoral applications for fintech, insurtech, telecoms and more. One recent successful collaboration was with deeptech startup Alphamoon, whose solution uses machine learning to automate document processing and classification. During development and implementation, Santander provided authentic data for AI training and validation, support for beta testing and feedback from business users, adaptation to the security standards of PFSA-regulated institutions, and promotional activities to help scale sales. As proof of its faith in Alphamoon, the bank became its first customer and now uses the tech to automate classification of customer complaints.

"We see fintechs as fully fledged participants in the service and financial products market," says Dawid. "These collaborations are an opportunity to improve our products and services and leverage new technologies, like those based on blockchain, which would simply be unprofitable for the bank to build from scratch. So we all benefit."

About

Santander Bank Polska is an active member of the Polish fintech support ecosystem and provides startups with valuable access to resources, data, testbeds and expertise to develop innovative services and products. Since 2019, the bank has run thirty joint proof-of-concept projects focusing on cybersecurity, payment tools, automation, Big Data, ecommerce and blockchain. Some twenty-five fintechs have also benefited from its accelerator program and the chance to test and adapt their solutions to the realities of a complex and highly regulated market.

[Contact]   Email: **dawid.galus@santander.pl** Telephone: **+48510028140**

[Links]   Web: **santander.pl/klient-indywidualny**
LinkedIn: **company/santander-bank-polska** Facebook: **santanderbankpolska**

"*We see fintechs as fully fledged participants in the service and financial products market. Collaborations are an opportunity to improve the products and services we offer our customers and leverage new technologies.*"

The Role of Collaboration in Fostering Innovation

Ewa Geresz / Director, Programs and Global Partnerships

Aureliusz Górski / Founding Executive Director

[Sector]   Industry agnostic

As an innovator or entrepreneur beginning your journey, you're often told that your path will be lonely and difficult or that any connections you do make will be based on the position you hold or the prestige of the company you work at. However, Venture Café Warsaw is turning this narrative around by making the entrepreneurs' journey one filled with two-way collaboration and authentic connections.

For Founding Executive Director Aureliusz Górski, an innovation-ecosystem facilitator, collaboration is how innovators and entrepreneurs can move from discussing a problem to taking action and solving it. He believes that in order to be a better collaborator, you must know your strengths and be aware of the situations in which you can truly shine and those in which you need to ask for help.

Venture Café Warsaw believes that innovation cannot happen behind closed doors. They encourage innovators to be unafraid when it comes to presenting their ideas at events and receiving feedback and guidance from other ecosystem players. In doing so, says Aureliusz, "we guarantee that you'll leave feeling more inspired and connected."

Programs and Global Partnerships Director Ewa Geresz, who is responsible for several programs aimed at strengthening the innovation environment in Poland and connecting it globally, agrees with Aureliusz that innovators must not isolate themselves. "Years ago," she says, "innovation was done in isolation." However, at the rate at which the world is changing, if you isolate yourself and shy away from collaboration, the world will leave you behind. "But when people of different backgrounds and from different industries gather together, they can look at issues from different, and from multiple, perspectives. That is when innovation can happen."

And that's why, she says, it is crucial for entrepreneurs to attend spaces and programs that facilitate conversations and collaborations with other innovators.

Most important tips for startups:

- **Attend the Thursday Gatherings.** These weekly gatherings are the core of the Innovation Campus and are always attended by incredible innovators of vastly different backgrounds. Attending these gatherings and collaborating with those you meet is the best way to get the most out of Venture Café Warsaw.

- **Keep an open mind.** Keeping an open mind and allowing oneself to communicate with people of different backgrounds is one of the most important qualities of a successful entrepreneur. New ideas can only be born out of communication with those that are different from you.

- **Focus on making real relationships.** Good networking is not about talking to as many people as you possibly can during an event. Instead, focus on cultivating real relationships that will last.

As an example that showcases how innovators can achieve success by attending spaces and events that foster collaboration, Ewa points to ForLogistic, a Polish company that offers express, short-term rental in the commercial real estate sector. "The founders met and came up with the idea behind ForLogistic during our virtual hackathon #IdeaHack," she says. "They then attended our Thursday gatherings and were able to meet other key members of their current team as well as their investors." Being open to sharing their ideas and talents with other innovators, and not being afraid to put themselves out there, allowed the founders of ForLogistic to create the first storage-industry platform in Poland and Europe based on the principle of the sharing economy (co-warehousing.)

"The spirit of collaboration," says Ewa, "is all about an exchange." In order to be better collaborators, you should be open to both receiving and giving help when it comes to innovation, and you must cultivate trust in your ecosystem. "Oftentimes, entrepreneurs are afraid of sharing their ideas and resources and of helping other innovators, because of negative experiences in the past." However, she explains, if there is a lack of social trust, and a belief that other innovators in your industry will not give back in the form of ideas, talent or resources, the collaboration will never be effective.

Of course, learning to trust others in your industry is sometimes easier said than done. One great strategy is to approach people and situations with an open mind and zero assumptions. "Every person that you meet," says Ewa, "should be looked at as a blank slate. You need to approach people with the intention to get to know them authentically and create friendships that will be beneficial to both sides." Once genuine friendships are established between entrepreneurs, the process of collaboration flows much more easily and naturally, and it is now based on a foundation of trust.

About

Venture Café Warsaw is a nonprofit organization and global network established in 2019. Beginning as a simple idea within the Cambridge Innovation Centre (CIC) in Massachusetts, the organization aims to connect innovators through high-impact programming and by providing spaces, storytelling, and broad-innovation engagement.

[Contact] Email: hello@venturecafewarsaw.org

[Links] Web: venturecafewarsaw.org LinkedIn: company/venturecafewarsaw
Facebook: venturecafewarsaw YouTube: VentureCafeWarsaw

" *Innovation happens when you share your story and collaborate with people of different backgrounds.* "

Helping Impactful Fintechs Introduce Innovative Solutions to Market

Igor Zacharjasz / Head, Digital Products & Innovation, Visa CEE

[Sector]   Technology

In unpredictable times like these, consumer needs and behaviors are changing faster than ever, so it's hard for service providers in any industry, let alone one as complex and security-focused as financial services, to keep up. Small, agile fintechs can successfully build up attractive offerings, but they need support in getting to market. Many fintechs scale quickly and don't always get the support they need. For a start, you need to amass the technological capabilities and capital to develop complex technology. Then you need to understand and navigate security challenges. And, finally, you must enter into partnerships with traditional market players. Getting a foothold in the market can be challenging for newcomers, which is why it's advisable to partner with an established financial institution to increase your chances of success.

Visa's Head of Digital Products and Innovation, Central Eastern Europe (CEE), Igor Zacharjasz, has over ten years' experience monitoring the financial sector to identify exciting new companies and solutions. As head of the Visa Innovation Studio, Warsaw, it's his job, among others, to seek out partnerships with fintech companies, as these are key to building innovations that benefit consumers, businesses and clients as well as the wider payments ecosystem.

Visa works closely with fintech companies of all sizes offering support, partnerships and investments as this collaboration can deliver exciting next-generation payment solutions to help make the world of payments better for consumers, businesses and communities. "Scouting for partners is a really important part of our job and Visa's strategy," says Igor. "We're looking for different partnerships, not just to fill our portfolio but to have a wider view of what's going on in the market."

Part of Visa's global network of Innovation Centers, the Warsaw Visa Innovation Studio, develops solutions to support the continuous growth of the digital economy in Poland. Project teams consist of experienced Visa experts and specialists assigned to specific projects by banks issuing Visa cards, as well as by acquirers.

A recent challenge tackled by the Studio focused on how banks and other financial institutions should communicate with senior citizens using mobile banking apps. This is a major issue in Poland where approximately one fourth of the population is aged sixty and over, with projections showing the percentage will grow to over 34% by 2040.[1]

Most important tips for startups:

- **Bring financial-sector experience to the table.** Established financial institutions won't deal with any company that doesn't know how to operate in this high-risk, strictly regulated market. To establish credibility and trust, at least one member of your C-level team should have financial sector experience.

- **Be ready to play a long game.** Selling to financial institutions takes much longer than in other industries – six to nine months as opposed to three or four – and decision-making processes are complex and drawn-out. You'll need sufficient capital, resources and patience to stay the distance.

- **Be agile and ready to adapt to changing demand.** Customer behavior is changing all the time, especially in uncertain times like these. You need to be flexible enough to turn threats into opportunities by reacting fast to changes in demand and behavior.

Key outcomes included the need to incorporate easy-to-find functionalities to initiate contact with banks through helplines, video calls or sign-language conversations; provide access to special offers meeting senior user needs; and facilitate remote support by family members.[2] The Studio also works on providing the framework of sustainability-related products and communications to Visa card-issuing banks and other financial institutions, including fintechs.

A successful project developed as part of one of the most notable Visa fintech programs, the Visa Fintech FastTrack, was carried out for Conotoxia, well known in Poland as Cinkciarz.pl, a major Polish multi-currency platform. This global fintech provides an extensive portfolio of financial services, including currency exchange, money transfer service, online payments, multi-currency cards and multi-currency lending services. Poland's large community of migrant workers, estimated at over 2.2 million[3] may find all of these services, in particular, the possibility of instant currency exchange, very useful.

The Fintech Partner Connect program supports Visa card-issuing customers and complements Visa's suite of value-added services. Another Visa offering dedicated to fintechs is the Developer Portal which offers direct access to a growing number of APIs, tools and support to help partners build easier, faster and more secure ways to power commerce.

Visa isn't new to working closely with the fintech sector and has a long history of championing new payments technology and working with fintechs as an investor and a partner. Indeed, in many ways, Visa is one of the original fintechs, with a sixty-year history of pioneering payments innovation – experience it puts to good use to help the sector grow further.

About

Visa is a world leader in digital payments, facilitating transactions between consumers, merchants, financial institutions and government entities in over two hundred countries. Via a network of partners, clients and entrepreneurs, Visa supports and invests in innovative fintechs to deliver next generation payment solutions for consumers, businesses and communities. As part of a global network, Visa Innovation Studio Warsaw develops solutions that drive the Polish digital economy, like card payments for micro-entrepreneurs, e-receipts and next-generation payments for smart city services and e-commerce.

---

[1]Statistics Poland (GUS), Senior citizens in Poland in 2020
[2]Qualitative research commissioned by Visa, sample of 22 adult Poles aged 60 years and over, 23 Jul – 10 Aug 2020
[3]Statistics Poland (GUS), Sizes and directions of Polish work migration 2004-2020

[Contact]   Email: biurowarszawa@visa.com   Telephone: +48221645600

[Links]   Web: visa.pl LinkedIn: company/visa Facebook: VisaPL Instagram: @visapl
Twitter: @VISA_PL

"Visa's mission is to remove barriers and connect more people to the global economy. Because we believe that economies that include everyone, everywhere, uplift everyone, everywhere."

foun

ders

Joanna Drabent

CEO, Cofounder / Prowly

One of Forbes' top European female founders, Jonna Drabent describes herself as an "accidental" PR expert whose first loves are filmmaking and art. After studying journalism and European studies at Warsaw University, a film festival internship led to her getting into media relations. She then gained experience working for PR firms before setting up her own agency, Kolko, in 2010, where the idea for Prowly was born. Since 2013, Joanna and cofounder Sebastian Przyborowski have grown Prowly into a trailblazing martech success. In 2020, they sold the company to Semrush.

How did the idea for Prowly come about?

My agency was responsible for handling media relations for Polish VC funds and startups. The startup scene had started to grow, and I was seeing brilliant ideas in other industries, technologies that were growing. And, like every entrepreneur, I wanted to improve my team's work. Other industries like sales or marketing have had dedicated software for some time, but we had to use universal solutions like Word or Excel for media relations activities. These were in no way adapted to our professional lives, and that's why I started thinking about such a tool. I called Sebastian – a brilliant web and app developer who I met in my first job – and we started thinking about what kind of software could improve daily media relations activities. We created an MVP and, after it launched, it turned out that the PR industry in Poland was willing to use it. It all happened a bit by accident. We've been running Prowly for over seven years now, and we're still here. We employ over fifty people and operate globally from Poland, but the majority of our customers are from the US.

You weren't tempted to try and develop the product in parallel with running Kolko?

No. When you're running a business based on services, and you need to grow the business with people and don't have your own product, this is a different business model. Prowly was a product company from the beginning. At the heart of our business is software that we're developing constantly. It would be really hard to connect the two. It's super difficult to scale an agency because the only way to grow is with people and clients. When you're running a software business, the challenge is totally different. It was also very exciting to grow my skills.

What have you learned?

The only thing I knew when we started was how to do PR properly. With Sebastian, we were a good team, because I know the industry well. I had enough of a network in Poland to get fast effective feedback. Sebastian was head of product from the beginning, and this connection was very good and is still working. Without this combination of skills, it would be really hard to succeed. Regarding the skills I have acquired, it's everything connected with scaling a software business. I've learned there's no secret sauce to make your company successful. Of course, you need to be hard working, have a strong personality and be patient. This kind of attitude, with a bit of luck, and a willingness to experiment and learn from mistakes, has helped us grow.

What competition do you face?

In Poland, there was one competitor when we started. Back then, we never thought we'd be able to grow Prowly on a global scale. We thought we would operate only in Poland. When it comes to the global market, there are lots of interesting players. It's growing rapidly. Considering the whole martech market, PR software is kind of niche, but there are very strong competitors, especially in the US.

You tried and failed to launch in the US. Why was that?

We had a traditional mindset back then. There wasn't a lot of experience we could use locally, because there weren't many SaaS companies operating globally. We thought we couldn't sell Prowly from Poland because of the language barrier, time difference, etc. But when you're running a software company, you've got remote in your DNA, and you don't need headquarters in San Francisco to sell effectively. But that was not our mindset in the beginning. We hired several people to grow our business in the US, and we failed because of lack of experience. We didn't have tested methodologies to scale our business that could be translated from the local to the US market. After three or four months, we decided to roll back and focus on creating internal processes, scaling the business and translating those processes outside Poland, and it turned out to be a successful approach. Now, after a few years, over fifty percent of our customers are based in the US. The Polish market is less than twenty percent. We're selling everywhere, from South Africa to Asia, North and South America, but the highest growth is in the US, and we do it all from here.

" *I learned entrepreneurship from my father, who taught me to see the world through the prism of challenges. Opportunities, not barriers.* "

What challenges did you face in the early days?

Funding was difficult because, in the last six years, I've become a wife and double mom. During my first pregnancy, we were closing one of the investment rounds in Poland. That was a big challenge because I felt I needed to convince the investor that I would be fine with being a mother and running a business, and they wanted me to translate such declarations into the investment agreement. That was hard because I don't feel I need to prove anything to anyone. But I wasn't that self-confident then, and I had some internal struggles. Finally, we closed the round and I proved to myself and the investor that my intuition was right.

How is it being a woman in a very male-dominated field?

Except for this, I haven't had any bad experiences. I learned entrepreneurship from my father, who taught me to see the world through the prism of challenges. Opportunities, not barriers. I don't consider I've struggled more because I'm a female founder. I'm quite stubborn and I like to act and follow my intuition, and when I learned that it works, I felt more self-confident. I believe everything comes from mindset. It's about not limiting yourself with "since I'm the woman, I will have it harder." If you think like this, you will see barriers everywhere.

Did you ever wonder if Prowly was going to make it?

I never felt we wouldn't make it; together with Sebastian, we call it a sense of survival. There were lots of moments we could say, "Okay, I'm done," without blaming ourselves. But we always had this strong belief that we need to succeed at some point. The biggest milestone was scaling outside Poland, because it took around two years to build the process for acquiring leads, and to grow our skills with closing deals, improving the app to sell more automatically, etc. There wasn't one reason we succeeded. It was a combination of experiments, starting from finding product market fit in the US through to optimizing the sales funnel, customer success, and helping our customers grow with our product.

You've landed some pretty big-name customers. Which are you most proud of having signed?

Spotify. That was the first recognizable customer. We started cooperating with them locally and then expanded in different markets. That was a big milestone because we connected the announcement with the launch of our new product we wanted them to use.

How did the Semrush exit come about?

That's another interesting story that happened by accident. In 2019, we were not looking to exit because we were in good shape. Semrush reached out to me to talk about business cooperation opportunities. They were looking for a PR software company that would fit into their product portfolio. After several calls and meetings with the team behind Semrush, our eyes were opened to the possibility of further development under the umbrella of one of the largest martech SaaS tools in the world. The whole process took a long time, over one year. In the meantime, I gave birth to my second child and the WHO announced the pandemic, and Poland and the US imposed lockdowns. That's why it took so long. But I felt comfortable because we didn't feel we needed to do it. We stayed calm and moved forward. In the meantime, we handled due diligence remotely. I will never forget scanning documents from my bedroom with two children with me. At the end of the day, we consider it an amazing opportunity to benefit from the experience of someone who has been where we were and to have the chance to develop our tool as a standalone brand and product in a direction that seemed natural for us.

So what's next?

Not much has changed. We stay as a standalone brand and entity, I'm still Prowly's CEO. We're now able to grow Prowly using the resources Semrush has opened up to us: experience and skills, as well as technologies to build other features connected with measuring the effectiveness of PR work. Our goal is to become an all-in-one PR solution. I'm super happy and excited that we can work on achieving this with such significant resources.

[About] Prowly is an all-in-one martech SaaS solution that optimizes the performance of media relations and saves time on routine tasks. The user-friendly platform lets PR professionals locate relevant media contacts and organize them in a customer-relationship management tool, create attractive press releases, send personalized pitches, and maintain a journalist-friendly newsroom.

[Links] Web: prowly.com LinkedIn: company/prowly-com Facebook: prowly Instagram: @prowly_com Twitter: @Prowly_com

What are your top work essentials?
Laptop, iPhone and Slack.

At what age did you found your company?
Twenty-seven.

What's your most used app?
The notes app on my phone. I like to make to-do lists.

What's the most valuable piece of advice you've been given?
Learn from your mistakes.

What's your greatest skill?
Not concentrating on the problem but on the opportunities and ways to solve it.

Jowita Michalska

Founder, CEO / Digital University

A Warsaw native, Jowita Michalska studied business management and marketing at the Warsaw School of Economics before embarking on a successful career in marketing and people-facing roles at big corporations such as Polkomtel, Deloitte and the Polish Energy Group. At thirty-five, when most people are settling comfortably into senior management and starting to think about their pension, she jumped ship to found an NGO, Digital University. Today, she's a dynamic member of Poland's tech and educational communities, organizing and speaking at conferences, startup weekends, hackathons and seminars. She's also a mentor, blogger and ambassador at Singularity University.

When did you get interested in tech and innovation?
My last full-time corporate job was as an advisor to the CEO of the biggest Polish energy company. A lot of responsibility. After that, I wanted to do completely different things, because I was a bit bored; the challenges are more or less similar. I was thinking about doing something that's good for people, meaningful. I also wanted to learn more about technology. While working in the telecom business, I understood technology was becoming more important. My first idea was to go to Stanford – I had a few friends there – stay a year, maybe learn a bit, learn about the community. But a friend said, "Instead of going to the US, let's bring them to Poland. Maybe someone else would like to learn about technology." So I went to board members in tech companies. That's the good thing when you start in big corporations and switch to a startup: you have relationships. I knew a lot of people. I went to them and said, "I want to start an NGO helping people learn about technology. Would you like to be a partner?" Some of them agreed, so we contacted different professors, starting with Harvard. The first was Professor Stefan Thomke, a Harvard innovation guru. We started giving free classes, partnered with the Warsaw School of Economics and brought in experts every two months. This was Digital University, and everyone wanted to come. In the first two years, over eight thousand people visited our classes and events, so it grew a lot.

Now you run it as a nonprofit and a business, correct?
Yes. I decided we should separate the NGO from the business, so I started the company. I had a private investor, a good friend who believes in education, so it was easy to work together. Now, Digital University is an NGO, and we focus on helping underprivileged people. Our biggest program helps young women from foster care.

We also teach kids the competencies of the future, and we're starting an ecology topic for primary schools in the smallest towns and villages in Poland. The for-profit company side provides technological education for businesses but is mostly focused on non-tech people, because it's important everyone understands what digital transformation means and what their role in the process is.

Is your offering unique in Poland, or do you have close competitors?

Something that differentiates us from competitors is that we focus on technology. So we're not only selling speakers, but we deeply understand the whole area and can help you go deep into the topic. There are lots of discussions about technology, but most businesses are still in the very early stages of adoption so they treat the topics on a very shallow level. So, there we can help. In Poland, I think our Speaker's Office is the biggest bureau, and we focus on tech speakers, which makes us popular. In the pandemic, learning and education became more important. Nobody wants an inspirational speaker from the TV who shares their life story; they want to learn practical skills. With educational programs, there are lots of competitors, but most are adult educational companies and they sell everything. Like, everyone sells stuff about leadership but we think about it differently. Digital leadership requires very different skills. So, a focus on being tech-savvy but also on empathy. Our digital transformation expert program is also unique. You can become a basic expert in the tech field after finishing it, and it's self-directed. It's really popular now because companies understand that if they have two, three or four hundred people who understand the basics of technology, it's much easier to transform.

Speaking of empathy, I imagine being a female-led tech-focused company is a big USP.

Absolutely, and it's not only me: almost the whole company is female. Only one man is working with us. When I talk to women, I give my example: I switched to something completely different aged thirty-five, learned something new and now I'm an expert in technology without having a tech background. This inspires them to say, "Okay, if she can do it, I can." I'm also raising women's voices at tech conferences where there are only a few women, and I say in the media that we need more women. I think it's extremely important to get more women on top in these areas. I'm also a mentor on many different programs.

"You have to focus not only on coming up with ideas but also on working hard and having the grit to deliver results."

What do you enjoy about mentoring?

I like that we work with different NGOs. Bianka Siwińśka from Perspektywy Women in Tech is a friend – we do a lot together – Olga Kozierowska from Sukces Pisany Szminką, Ela Raczkowska from Vital Voices. I work with them and for them, and they work with me and for me. Mentorship is something that inspires me. I try to make young women understand that they are stronger, that they can do it. I see it when we work with women from foster care. The problem isn't teaching them technology; it's helping them believe in themselves. I think I have very balanced self-esteem, which I had to learn, and I want to share it, give them some inspiration. The university program came about because I was thinking about how to dedicate my time as precisely as possible. I wanted to work with people who, if they didn't meet someone like me, maybe would never do anything unusual or interesting. Everyone said we shouldn't do it, it's too difficult, adults from foster care are too complicated... but I'm happy we didn't listen. Fifty percent of them, at least, have changed their lives completely. They were being forced by the system to become hairdressers, shop assistants, and being told they weren't good enough, and now some go to university, become junior developers, digital marketers. But it's tricky because, due to lack of self-esteem, sometimes they resign. So we have psychologists on the program, and they can come back to us for three years afterward to ask for help.

You've got a lot to be proud of. What stands out the most?

Switching sides at thirty-five. Giving up everything I did before, which was successful, convenient and well paid to do what I wanted. I'm proud that I am open to change. It's natural for me and I'm not afraid of new things. I proved myself in different areas, and I'm still open to new ones.

What have been your biggest challenges along the way?

Finding and keeping great talent, which is always difficult if you don't have diversity (I'm working on that). Persuading them to join us, not Google, for example. Keeping them and creating a culture of innovation and openness. Also, scaling a business in such changing times. Deciding which areas to get involved in next. And growing, because we move really fast. Also, we spend time with the smartest people in the world, which is great, but very challenging.

How does being in Warsaw help your business?

We have a lot of big tech companies and budgets here, and it's important to know them and work where the money is. Friends that come here from the US say, "Oh, your innovation is very new," and I like that. When you go to the coworking spaces over there, they're old. In Poland, though, it's nice to work somewhere like CIC coworking. The community is vibrant, and people are very open. There's also a lot of diversity here. We have great talent, really smart people, dedicated, desperate to learn as much as possible.

What advice do you have for other entrepreneurs?

I think we are forced by the media to think you have to find your true passion and that's the most important thing, but it's not true. You have to focus not only on coming up with ideas but also on working hard and having the grit to deliver results. That's the most important thing. Many people have great ideas, but only a few can survive in this very difficult world. Ego is another thing: All these young startup founders have huge egos, and it's often the biggest problem because you won't retain talent if your ego is too big. I've seen many brilliant companies with brilliant products dying because of the founder's ego. Finally, especially in tech, be a constant learner. Make time for learning because in this world your only advantage is to learn faster than the rest.

[About] Digital University collaborates with world-renowned speakers and experts from the worlds of business and science to run conferences and offer broad-ranging education about digital technologies and digital transformation for business leaders, entrepreneurs, students, public administration managers and underprivileged groups. Digital University also represents the Singularity University in Warsaw.

[Links] Web: digitaluniversity.pl LinkedIn: company/digitaluniversity
Facebook: digitaluniversitypoland Instagram: @_digital_university_

What are your top work essentials?
My Mac and someone to talk with and bounce ideas off.

At what age did you found your company?
Thirty-five.

What's your most used app?
Pocket, Spotify, Apple podcast.

What's the most valuable piece of advice you've been given?
Be selective about who and what you dedicate your time to.

What's your greatest skill?
I'm a good communicator, storyteller and networker, and I'm very persuasive.

Marcin Beme

Founder, CEO / Audioteka

A Warsaw native, Marcin Beme studied economics, math and computer science at Warsaw University and Warsaw University of Technology. After founding startups in the telecoms and media sectors, he got into creating audiobook content in 2011, which led to the foundation of Audioteka. Despite a challenging start, he and his cofounder succeeded in creating a market for what proved to be a highly successful business model. Today, Marcin is no longer involved in Audioteka's day-to-day operations and is focusing instead on closing the biggest funding round of his career for his next groundbreaking venture involving content, NFTs and gaming. His contributions to advancing digital technologies, entrepreneurship and Polish culture have been recognized by the likes of *Forbes*, *Business Insider* and the Polish government, among many others.

How did you get into the media and tech sectors?

After I finished my studies, I dreamed of becoming a venture capitalist. It was all about money, investing, building stuff, etc. I literally believed I would finish my studies and launch my own VC fund. As you can imagine, it was not that easy to graduate and get people's money without any track record, so I ended up on the other side and started my first business. I was invited by my colleague to join him in a technology company producing software and hardware for wireless data transmission. It was a long time ago, but today you would call it an IoT sector. We produced our own hardware and software that enabled devices, ATMs, gauges and electricity, gas meters, etc. to be managed online, remotely. That was the first venture. We sold it, and then the second venture was closer to Audioteka. It was a TV production company, which gave me the first experience of doing business with content. I learned that you either own the IP or control the distribution channel. The TV production company wasn't a big success, but it was the best school to learn the media business. After that, I started Audioteka, which connected the dots from my two previous businesses (because it was all about managing IP for a certain type of content – first audiobooks and then audio in general) and a bit of the experience I had in the technology company, because Audioteka was very strongly technological, at least at the beginning.

And why audiobooks? Where did the idea come from?

It was from when I was very intensely training in kite surfing at the Polish seaside, so I was traveling with my brother almost every weekend. From Warsaw, the seaside is a five-hundred-kilometer drive, so we were totally bored during those trips and we started to listen to audiobooks. On CDs, of course. And the other angle of how the audiobook idea landed on my table was that my colleague, a brilliant sound engineer, approached me with an idea to build a publishing house to put audiobooks on CDs. He had some contacts with the state-owned Polish radio, which has lots of archives. We were discussing the concept over dinner at my place, and my girl, now my wife, said, "Guys, this makes no sense to do CDs. You should put it on the internet." And I thought this was the most stupid idea, because I was about to exit the TV-production company. We were switching from TV to content production because TV production had stopped being a business; it became a commodity. It was very difficult, it became very competitive, and we had started to invest in internet shows because every TV production company has a problem of delivering services to a very limited number of clients. Here in Poland, we had public TV and two private stations. There was no growth story, so we started to look for other ways to produce something for ourselves and build our own channels. And it was twenty years ago, so there weren't any internet shows, no Netflix, not even social media. It was much too early, and the content we put on the internet was a disaster because there was no viewership, no technology for people to watch it. So when I heard "Let's put some content on the internet," I was not too enthusiastic. But my conscience said we have to do it, so we did. This was in 2011.

Also, I was never a strong reader – I was always the sports guy, always on the move – and maybe I did it subconsciously for all the people who are not strong readers. And it changed my life, because I consumed a lot of books I would never have consumed.

What other challenges did you face early on? And how did you overcome them?

We were way ahead of the market. In the first years, there were no sales. Of course, in the US, Audible was already very big, and Amazon was already acquiring it; there was a market. But in Europe, audiobooks were for blind people and kids. They were not a sexy product, so the market was not there. The biggest struggle was to change perceptions. And our stubbornness, consistency and focus saved us, and a belief that we were doing this not only for money because I truly believe we can have some impact on the universe. I mean, we're a small company, but I believe that with our abilities, and the money we have access to, we can make a change.

"Understand technology deeply. Because even if you do business in culture, it's still technology driven, so you have to understand tech."

At a certain moment, it started to take off. Of course, apps became normal. The first app we created was for Nokia. I managed to make the huge Nokia corporation have our application installed on Nokia phones, so we got over a million phones where our application was just a click away. That made us push ahead. Second, huge creativity on the content-creation side, because we created a format that I call super-production. We started to promote it as not just audiobooks but an audio experience, using actors and music to produce our content – moving away from books but towards listening – and it was a much wider market. These were two turning points in our history.

Of course, both had hiccups. We made apps for all devices, even those that didn't exist, because we wanted to be everywhere. It cost a lot of money, and lots of those apps died; only the Apple and Android ones remain. And super-production costs a lot of money. It's ten times more expensive than traditional audiobooks, so we really had to believe that it was going to pay off.

You were pretty visionary, then?

Yes. There was a feeling I never had, before or after. I just saw ahead, to be honest. I can't explain it, but I just knew what would happen, step by step. I didn't know exactly, but the direction was so clear to me. Of course, this isn't rocket science or a cure for cancer, but we had a pretty good feeling about what we're doing. As I said before, it's about believing why we were doing it, because in the beginning, it was totally not about money. It wasn't making any money. The start especially was very difficult.

What advice do you have for other founders?

Believing is fundamental. Understanding why you do it. If you ask yourself, "Why am I doing this?" and the answer is, "To make some money," maybe that's not the best answer – maybe you're wasting your time a bit. So, believe what you do, look for some real problem solving, and mind the market. The audiobook market was very small, and building a market takes time. So, understand why you do it, look for solutions to real problems, check the solutions are solving a problem for a market which is big enough.

Today, everything happens very quickly compared to before, so if you want to grab a chance, you have to act super quickly, both spending money, hiring people, firing people, testing your idea, verifying. These are completely different times now. You can bootstrap almost anything these days. And, of course, understand technology deeply. Because even if you do business in culture, it's still technology driven, so you have to understand tech. It must become part of your DNA.

Warsaw is a good place to hire tech talent. Are there any other advantages to being here?
Warsaw and Poland had an advantage some time ago because we had good talent, especially in technology, and it was not so expensive, so it was quite different starting in Warsaw versus Munich, for example. Now, it has completely changed because of the pandemic. Remote working became normal and prices are more or less equal, which is good because taking advantage of cheap people isn't a very good and sustainable advantage. On the other hand, when you open up from this perspective, you also open up for business people, which Poland was never very strong at. It's starting now. Other colleagues more successful than me built and sold their companies, and they're investing back. There's experience being built on the technological level but also on the business level, especially in digital, because we don't have many people who have succeeded in this area from Poland, from Warsaw. But there are more and more coming in and getting back on the market. It's very important that they contribute their money and experience.

[About]   Audioteka is the largest audiobook and non-musical audio-content producer in the CEE region, producing, sourcing, selling and distributing audiobooks, dramas and podcasts. Content is available via Audioteka's own digital platform and apps – as well as third-party mobile apps, internet-enabled vehicles and smart speakers – in eight countries and eleven languages.

[Links]   Web: audioteka.com Facebook: audioteka Instagram: @audioteka
Twitter: @audioteka

What are your top work essentials?
My phone, my Mac and my headphones, of course.

At what age did you found your company?
Twenty-eight.

What's your most used app?
Windguru (for kite-surfing), Snow-Forecast (for skiing),
Google apps (for work).

**What's the most valuable piece of advice you've
been given?**
Understand why you're doing what you're doing and
believe in it.

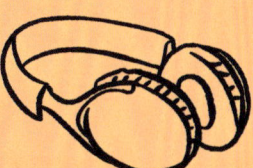

What's your greatest skill?
Making things happen, giving energy to others, creating
stuff from nothing.

Paweł Sieczkiewicz

Founder, CEO / Telemedi

Originally from Siedlce, Poland, Paweł Sieczkiewicz began his studies in business management at Warsaw University of Technology but was ejected from his course after the first year for dedicating too much of his time to his budding software-development company. After meeting his Telemedi cofounder at Startup Weekend, the business evolved from general SaaS solutions to telemedicine software. In 2014, they launched Telemedi as a virtual clinic to provide advanced digital healthcare solutions for patients. Paweł did eventually finish his studies part time at Kozminski University, and today Telemedi continues to go from strength to strength. In addition to masterminding the company's global expansion, Paweł has been listed five times in *Forbes* 30 Under 30 and is a mentor and regular speaker at events.

Why did you move from general software development to telemedicine?
I met my cofounder. All his family were doctors, and he came up with the idea that it would be great to give the doctors the ability to charge for online consultations, like telephone consultations with patients, and for patients to directly be able to book, pay and feel comfortable talking to doctors. Startup Weekend is an event where people meet other people with ideas or who can develop these ideas, and they develop their prototype of the possible solution, possible companies. And we are an example of such cooperation, and we went forward. But after three years, my cofounder said it wasn't growing as fast as he imagined, and he left the company. I continued developing it, and our biggest growth happened four years ago, so around one and a half years after he left the company.

Why was growth so slow those few first years?
During the first years, there was a problem mostly with finding product-market fit, because individual patients didn't want to pay for such a service. When we were testing patient satisfaction, they were very satisfied with the online presentations they were getting; but when we asked them to pay for it, they didn't want to, even when we were testing different pricing ranges, like five, ten, fifteen, twenty, fifty złoty. So we realized there wasn't such a big difference in conversion rates depending on the price. The main difference was when we wanted to charge or give it for free. So this intention to pay was the most important blocker. Then, we found out that we could take such solutions to B2B companies that would pay for our services and offer them to their customers. So we are working with B2B. An individual patient can pay for our services, but mostly we're focusing on the B2B segment. And there are sub-segments, like banks, insurance companies, assistance companies, etc.

They are merging our portfolio for their patients or their customers, giving it as an additional value, for example, to bank accounts or insurance products. Or their insurance products include health care products, and they want to give online consultations and physical visits as an added value.

How have you handled the process of expanding to other countries?
We've moved into other countries first in a light model. So we started to hire doctors in other languages, started to talk to clients in other regions. And now we are moving into other countries with a full rollout model and starting on-ground operations. We have started already in Spain, and right now we are rolling out to Germany. Next year we are launching in new countries in Europe and Latin America.

What challenges does that bring?
Medicine itself is challenging because every country has slightly different regulations. After that, the market has different needs, so we need to customize our approach to different markets to cover these needs with our infrastructure. After Poland, we've chosen the countries where we think there's a best fit and opportunity. That's why we chose Spain, and we already got good signals there, a few clients on board. We have two models of expansion: this light model, and we have deals in twenty countries, and then we get some signals and go for on-ground rollout.

How have you funded it all?
First, with my cofounder, with our own money. After that, we joined Wayra Accelerator. Then a few business angels came on board later. DocPlanner has also invested in us. Then we started to work with VCs to develop our growth. Black Pearls VC funded our seed round. Then we raised Series A, led by Flashpoint, UNIQA VC, PKO VC, and Black Pearls, for €5.5 million, which we're using for IT development and launch in new countries. IT, marketing, and sales expansion to new countries is the most cash-hungry part of our business. Right now, Telemedi is coordinating two worlds: the world of online consultations (telemedicine) and the world of physical visits (physical medical services in one place). Our B2B clients can do everything related to health and have it in one dashboard. So we are digitalizing healthcare, not just telemedicine. Our product has grown. We take care of all the everyday processes: going to the doctor, physical visits, lab tests, online consultations... and we are coordinating between many doctors and many, many clinics. We've already integrated one thousand labs and over seventy physical clinics and we are moving forward with more.

"*Doing the same things in the same way will not get you different results.*"

Has the pandemic and the move to doing everything online helped public acceptance?

We're focusing on B2B, so digitalization in healthcare is a strong megatrend, but from the individual patient's perspective, it definitely helped. Now, either you have used telemedicine or you know someone who has. It's very popular right now and has educated the market, and it's pushing our B2B clients to think about digitalization even more. Health insurance companies are usually the first movers taking innovations to the market. They are looking for things to offer, to optimize the process. Once it's rolled out to private insurance companies, public administrations follow. They are very risk-averse and looking for validated solutions. If it wasn't for big companies like insurance testing these solutions, there would be no innovations in the public sector.

What have been some milestones along the way?

First, finding product-market fit and that our B2B clients loved us. Second, getting new clients on board, because the insurance industry is very risk-averse, and our portfolio shows we are already the leading company in terms of the trust they have in us. Also, when Telemedi evolved from a telemedicine company to a healthcare company, when we started to integrate and coordinate the physical world with online treatment.

Do you have many competitors?

Many competitors are focusing on individual patients and digital health, and this is a much bigger market than what we are doing. We are focusing on our narrow case, being a partner for B2B clients, and there aren't many companies taking this exact approach. Some companies are trying to do B2C plus our approach, but we're winning in terms of B2B clients and being the top-of-mind partner.

What would you do differently, knowing what you know now?

We went down the VC path quite late. It would have been better to do it faster. At the same time, the VC sector wasn't so big in Poland five or ten years back. I would also grow the team faster because we achieved a lot with a small team, but it would probably be better to do it with a bigger team.

How has your team grown over the years? Is it easy finding the talent you need?

Right now, we have around 140 people taking care of the platform and around 600 doctors. Last year, we grew to around eighty to ninety people. We do two things: The first, everyone does, which is pay well. Second, we offer additional value, because in telemedicine you are helping patients who already need healthcare but, as a young person, you are helping optimize healthcare for the time when you will need it.

What does a city like Warsaw offer for a business like yours?

Compared to other countries, there are positives and negatives. The negative is that it's easier to launch new companies when you have access to people who already had great success in the startup world. Until now, we didn't have so many global successes in Poland. But it's changing, people are exiting companies, starting new companies, recruiting new people who, by osmosis, are learning great ways of building startups. We are lacking a lot of great people here in Warsaw, but in post-COVID times it shouldn't be a barrier to expanding a company because we shouldn't only look for Warsaw-based people. You need to have a country where you are comfortable living because you can work from anywhere. The most important thing is the ratio of value-for-money living in Warsaw. And great infrastructure. Founders cannot think in terms of cities anymore; we are a global village. Where you are based isn't the most important factor anymore. Now it's not only Warsaw-based companies competing for Warsaw talent. It's not related to the city anymore. Warsaw is good for flights to Europe and other countries, and the living costs are fine.

Any advice for other entrepreneurs?

Facts, not opinions. Also, doing the same things in the same way will not get you different results.

[About]   Telemedi is a B2B white-label digital health platform provider. It allows clients to offer their own B2C customers a range of remote and in-person healthcare services including medical consultations, lab tests, medical device monitoring and more.

[Links]   Web: telemedi.com LinkedIn: company/telemedi-co Twitter: @telemedi_co

What are your top work essentials?
My phone, Google Meet and the time of better people than me.

At what age did you found your company?
Twenty-one.

What's your most used app?
Google Meet, Notes, Calendar, Google Docs.

What's the most valuable piece of advice you've been given?
Building an organization is different to building a business.

What's your greatest skill?
Connecting the dots.

Vadym Melnyk

CEO, Founder / Dronehub

Originally from Ukraine, Vadym Melnyk was interested in robotics from an early age, winning several national and international competitions while still in high school, both in Europe and in the US during a scholarship. He went on to study computer engineering at the University of Information Technology and Management in Rzeszów, Poland, where he started collaborating with Microsoft. He founded Cervi Robotics (later rebranded as Dronehub) in his final year and dropped out before graduation to focus on scaling the company. In 2020, he was listed in *Forbes* 25 Under 25, proving you don't need a degree to be successful.

What did you gain from being Microsoft's student partner?
Microsoft was supporting young leaders. We were giving speeches at national and international conferences, learning cutting-edge Microsoft technologies, so it was really cool. We built our name, our credibility, thanks to Microsoft.

You were also Chief of its Unicorn Division, right?
I had a choice to become the regional leader or create something new, so I decided to create something new: a program to support young startups, match them with venture capital, and give them Microsoft Cloud, everything Microsoft can do for startups in Central and Eastern Europe. In the beginning, the name was fairly corporate and boring, and I negotiated to change it because I wanted to have a business card saying "Unicorn Division." I had a group of interesting, outstanding people working with me, scouting interesting startups, mostly in software. By then, I had lots of experience with startups. I'd won lots of different competitions and knew lots of venture capitalists and business angels, and how to scout startups. It was basically my experience and knowledge that led to the creation of this program.

Tell me about the early days of Cervi Robotics.
In 2015, we were doing custom drones for defense, police and large enterprises. It started growing very well, but at some point we lost focus. We were doing lots of things connected with robotics, but they were factory automation, Industry 4.0 projects. Basically, outsourcing for large corporations and getting very good revenue. In 2017, we received our first large contract from the European Space Agency, which also works with the low space where airplanes and drones fly. They needed a solution where a drone can land autonomously without an operator and change the battery, and they chose us as joint partners.

In 2017, we built our first working prototype. The best thing about cooperating with these public agencies is that the IP stays in the company. We had a tough decision: focus on what we were doing, like outsourcing, or build a new product. That's when we started investing all the money we earned into Dronehub. In 2019, after some large grants, some private investments and our own money, we built a fully working product. Our first customer was PKN Orlen, the largest oil and gas company in Central and Eastern Europe. We sold the Dronehub system to automate monitoring of critical infrastructure in their Płock refinery, and it was a big success. After that, we started getting more customers. In January 2020, we decided to refuse all contracts not connected to Dronehub and focus purely on automated drone platforms and the software.

Because you thought Dronehub would be more profitable?
No. In January 2020, we had contracts for almost three million złoty for outsourcing, robotics and drones, but not connected with Dronehub. It was a very hard decision because at the time we had only one customer. But we realized we had something unique, something which solves a real problem. We had a few potential competitors in the US and Israel, but we were far ahead of them. We decided it was the ideal moment to focus on the product and build a product company. Time has shown that it was a bold but good decision. Today we are the leader of drone-in-a-box systems in Europe.

Why were you so far ahead of the pack?
We were solving a real problem from the very beginning, and we had a real customer, the European Space Agency, which helped us make the right decisions. When we started working with them, we received a grant for just over one million euros from the European Commission to work on autonomous hubs, but for cargo deliveries. When we finished in 2020, we were the only company in the world that had this three-in-one drone infrastructure for different kinds of missions: stationary monitoring, mobile monitoring and cargo deliveries. Also, we didn't create a closed ecosystem. We want to integrate with all drones on the market. This is our competitive advantage because our competitors have to focus on everything from software, through mobile and ground infrastructure, to drones, legislation and sales. We don't have to focus on absolutely everything because our drone partners are doing that and we just integrate with them, so it helps us iterate faster.

If you want to learn to do business, do services: outsourcing, a software house, something like that. But if you want to build a product, do that from the start.

What challenges have you faced?

Like they say, "the hardware is very hard." We had lots of problems building a robust product that works one hundred percent of the time. If we build a drone station and the drone lands forty-nine times out of fifty, that's not enough. We had to do eight iterations, which cost a lot. Every iteration is €200,000 to €250,000. We put a lot of money into R+D. The challenge we're facing right now is certification, because we are starting to sell to the defense and military market and the number of certificates you need is enormous. But our biggest issue is sales. Our sales funnel is very long, between six to nine months. So, we've started working on the cloud platform to automate data processing, and we'll release the first public beta in January 2022. This will give us more predictable revenue. We'll be bringing in partners not only for the ground infrastructure, which they usually buy once, but also for software.

What fundraising have you done?

In 2020, when we decided to focus purely on Dronehub, we closed an investment round for 2.2 million złoty from VC and business angels. In late 2020, Dronehub received a $1.9 million grant from the Polish National Centre for Research and Development to create mobile drone infrastructure for automatic orthophotos (aerial photos). Now, the Polish Agency for Enterprise Development has given us a grant for eleven million złoty to build our factory and go from low-level to mass production, building up around five hundred docking stations per year. We're also closing a VC round for four million euros, late seed or A round. Right now, we can only make a few dozen hubs per year. Now, we'll be able to manufacture five to six hundred, more than enough since one hub sells for around €100,000.

What have been your biggest milestones?

Winning *Forbes* 25 Under 25 and switching from outsourcing to building my own product. Previously, I was afraid to do that, because services are more predictable. With a product, you need to invest a lot first, and you're not sure if in the end there will be something profitable. Now, Dronehub is one of the leaders, not regionally but internationally, with this autonomous drone technology. I'm very happy that at twenty-seven, I have built a company doing something unique.

What do you like about being in Warsaw?

It's good for networking because all of the large corporates and public institutions – most of our Polish clients – are here. We opened our Warsaw office in 2020. In February 2021, when we grew big, we relocated to the Varso Tower complex, so Dronehub is now at the very center of the Polish business, startup and innovative environment. I have my management and sales teams here, and we move forward quickly with deals.

Our headquarters for R+D and production is in Rzeszów, South-Eastern Poland, at the heart of the Aviation Valley, so it's easy to get top-quality engineers. Warsaw is a good place to look for talented C-level managers. It's a perfect place for business, because the cost of living versus the quality of employees is better than, say, the Netherlands, which is more expensive. Another good thing in Poland is the amount of support money from the European Commission and the National Centers for Research and Development. Without that, we wouldn't be where we are now, because the amount of money here for A, B, and C rounds is limited compared to the US, Israel or Western Europe. There's tons of money for seed, usually €250,000 to €300,000, but you can't do a lot with that.

Why does Poland lack venture capital?
It's complex, but Poland has been a free-market economy for only thirty years, after half a century of communism. There aren't many large private companies that have generated huge amounts of money and been here for generations, like family offices in the US or UK.

Any advice for other entrepreneurs?
If you want to learn to do business, do services: outsourcing, a software house, something like that. But if you want to build a product, do that from the start. Most entrepreneurs think "I'll start by building a software company, do some outsourcing, earn money, gain experience, and then build my own product."
In my experience, that usually never happens. I have a dozen friends who started software houses, and now it's too hard for them to switch from outsourcing to product. So, if you want to build a product, build a product, and have a customer who won't just pay you but can tell you if you're moving in the right direction.

[About]   Dronehub is a world-leading manufacturer of innovative drone-in-a-box solutions, including drones, mobile ground infrastructure and AI-powered software. Its drones are capable of performing 24/7 missions without human intervention, including monitoring, inspection, measurement and cargo transport. Dronehub partners with IBM and cooperates with the European Space Agency and European Defense Agency.

[Links]   Web: dronehub.ai LinkedIn: company/dronehubgroup Facebook: DronehubGroup
Twitter: @DronehubGroup

What are your top work essentials?
Laptop, smartphone, passport and Internet access,
because I travel a lot.

At what age did you found your company?
Twenty.

What's your most used app?
Gmail, but I hate it. My favorite app is Things.

**What's the most valuable piece of advice you've
been given?**
It's better to lose with a smart person than win with
a stupid one.

What's your greatest skill?
One, I never have a hangover from tequila. Two, I have
a talent for finding the right people at the right place
and time.

ools

- Be ready for a selective, albeit short, application process.
  Admission is based on two criteria: GPA on your previous studies and results of an online entry test.

- Show keen interest in your chosen field of study.
  Candidates are expected to possess some basic knowledge of the area they plan to explore.

- Have values rooted in ethics and integrity.
  The curriculum encompasses many diverse business, legal and management topics, with the school committed to ingraining and nourishing the highest ethical standards and a good business sense in students.

- Put common good before all else.
  Together with forty-six universities from all over the world, KU was included in the Positive Impact Rating (PIR) and expects students to have similar mindsets.

[Name]

Kozminski University

[Elevator Pitch]
"We are a business-oriented higher education institution offering a broad range of Polish- and English-language programs in management, law, finance and economy. We rank among the best business schools in Europe, according to the Financial Times."

[Enrollment]
Total enrollment: 10,000 (2022)

[Description]
Founded in 1993, Kozminski University (KU) is a business-oriented higher education institution offering a broad range of education programs, holding full academic rights. It is known as one of the oldest non-public higher education institutions in Poland and prides itself on having obtained three prestigious international accreditations: AACSB, EQUIS and AMBA, held by only one hundred business schools worldwide.The university aims to implement technological innovations alongside its standard teaching processes. By using solutions based on AI, VR and gamification, among other technological advances, it shares knowledge and combines it with immersive, thought-provoking experiences for its staff and students.

The school's diversity is reflected through its partnership with 220 educational institutions around the world. Many classes at KU are taught by academics from various countries, and about one thousand students take part in exchange programs throughout the year. The school's faculty members also lecture and conduct research at many other well-known universities abroad, including Harvard, MIT and ESCP Business School. The education and general development of those at the university are further supported with the help of tools and licenses to develop students' professional skills alongside their problem-solving and decision-making abilities. For example, KU students have unlimited access to the LinkedIn learning platform offering 12,000 online courses in various areas, and both students and graduates can use the *Financial Times* website as premium users.

KU's curriculum straddles the highest academic standards of research and practical applications in the business and organizational milieus. In addition, students participate in extended internship programs at the top companies, institutions and organizations in Poland and abroad. The school is also committed to sustainable development and has been placed among some of the world's leaders of positive change, committed to ingraining and nourishing the highest ethical standards and a good business sense in its students, professors and staff.

[Apply to]
kozminski.edu.pl/en/programs

[Links]
Web: **kozminski.edu.pl/en** LinkedIn: **school/akademialeonakozminskiego**
Facebook: **kozminski** Instagram: **@kozminskiuniversity** Twitter: **@KozminskiUni**
YouTube: **kozminski**

- **Be entrepreneurially oriented.**
  Starting a business requires risk-taking, and here at SGH, we want to prepare our students to take those risks as intelligently as possible.

- **Have completed undergraduate university studies.**
  SGH's curriculum is rigorous, and students are best prepared by having already obtained an academic degree.

- **Have a minimum of three years of professional experience.**
  Here at SGH, we believe that those who succeed have a combination of world-class education and hands-on experience.

- **Be fluent in English.**
  International business is often conducted in English, and setting our students up for success means preparing them to conduct themselves in English.

[Name]
SGH Warsaw School of Economics

[Elevator Pitch]
"We are one of Poland's top business schools. We're proud to announce our MBA for Startups, Poland's first online program designed especially for young entrepreneurs."

[Enrollment]
Total enrollment: 40 students per year

[Description]
The SGH Warsaw School of Economics, founded in 1906, is Poland's oldest business school. The innovative university is focused on developing creative and intellectual potential and educating leaders in response to the challenges of the future. SGH was ranked the number-one economics university in Poland by the Polish newspaper *Rzeczpospolita* (in 2019) and by the education foundation Perspektywy (in 2021), and it has been listed in the *Financial Times* as one of the best Masters in Management. Like many innovative companies around the world, SGH has been adapting to the COVID-19 pandemic. It now has an international program that will remain available fully online.

SGH's MBA for Startups, which aims to attract a younger cohort of entrepreneurs than some of its other MBA programs do, is specifically focused on the aspects of starting a business as opposed to maintaining an already established corporate position. "We decided to do something completely new," says Rafal Mrowka, director of the MBA Program Office. "The MBA for Startups is focused on students who want to start small companies. It's a different curriculum, all related to starting a business. It's also a fully online program."

Among the many highlights of the curriculum is the capstone project in which students develop an innovative business idea as a group. The project involves pitching the idea to senior faculty to help develop students' ability to sell their business ideas. SGH's program has many corporate partners, including Sebastian Kulczyk, Poland's wealthiest businessman. The program even features Kulczyk's InCredibles mentoring program wherein students are matched with an array of international mentors who provide advice and guidance throughout the two-year program. "We have a lot of great partners from the startup community," says Rafal, "including investors who have already had success in the startup world and are experienced in it. The program is very practical."

[Apply to]
sgh.waw.pl / mbaforstartups.pl

[Links]
Web: **sgh.waw.pl** LinkedIn: **school/sgh-warsaw-school-of-economics** Facebook: **SGHwarsaw**
Instagram: **@sghwarsaw** Twitter: **@SGHWarsaw**

- **Have a strong educational background.**
  We place excellence at the heart of what we do and want our applicants to have a strong educational background with a very good command of English.

- **Be open to the world.**
  We attract students from across the globe and want our students to be open-minded and willing to learn from other cultures.

- **Demonstrate passion and commitment.**
  We want our students to demonstrate a passion and commitment to their chosen subject area. Our courses and programs are demanding, and our students should be able to show that they are ready for the challenge.

- **Present yourself professionally.**
  We pride ourselves on offering a high quality education to all our students, and we expect our students to take their academic endeavours seriously and to present themselves professionally.

[Name]
University of Warsaw, Faculty of Management

[Elevator Pitch]

"Our Faculty of Management is a place where knowledge meets practice and a space for innovation and entrepreneurship. We teach our students how to responsibly manage a business using modern tools and methods that can be applied across global markets."

[Enrollment]

Total enrollment : 40,200 (2020)
Faculty of Management: 5,000 (2020)

[Description]

Established in 1816, the University of Warsaw is Poland's largest university and is recognized across the globe as one of the leading academic institutions and research centers in Europe. Since its beginning, it has played a pivotal role in the cultural, intellectual and political life of Poland. It is also home to six Nobel Prize winners and the famous pianist Chopin attended the university. It consistently appears in the global league tables as one of the best universities in the world and is frequently rated in first or second place in the Polish rankings. There are twenty-four faculties and thirty academic units, and students can choose from more than two hundred different programs of study. It offers twenty-eight programs in English and has a broad range of subject areas, from archaeology, culture and arts to geology, modern languages, physics, psychology and many more.

The Faculty of Management, founded in 1972, is the oldest business school in Poland and the CEE region. Each year, it attracts over five thousand students to its programs and is accredited by EQUIS and AMBA. Students can opt to major in either management or finance, and the faculty has a strong and rigorous focus on theory combined with practical work. There is a mandatory internship and options to study abroad. The faculty runs three unique programs: the International Business Program, the Global MBA and the Executive MBA. The Global MBA is a flagship program run in collaboration with three other international partners. Students get the opportunity to attend all four universities, gaining unparalleled international experience and learning from academic leaders in their field. Across all three programs, there is a strong focus on intercultural communication and international management practices. The Faculty is currently in the process of joining the Association to Advance Collegiate Schools of Business (AACSB), one of the most prestigious accreditations in the world.

[Apply to]

irk.uw.edu.pl/en-gb

[Links]

Web: **wz.uw.edu.pl/en** LinkedIn: **school/wydzial-zarzadzania-uniwersytet-warszawski**

- **Be clear on your motivations.**
We offer a selection of different programs, each with its own unique expectations and requirements, and we pride ourselves on having a tough selection process. We advise you to ask questions to clarify your expectations before applying.

- **Talk to us.**
Do your research and compare us to our competitors. Read about our alumni's experiences. Reach out and talk to us. This way you can be absolutely sure that our programs are right for you. We are looking for those who are sure about their desire to join us.

- **Be yourself.**
We are looking out for a personality match and not just qualifications. Approach us and be yourself.

- **Bring your work experience to the table.**
Extensive experience in the workplace is highly recommended. We accept candidates with various backgrounds and working experience, but for some programs managerial experience is preferred.

[Name]
Warsaw University of Technology Business School

[Elevator Pitch]
"We educate flexible, responsible, competent and versatile business leaders who can adapt to even the most volatile and uncertain business environment and who understand the role and potential of new technologies in modern management."

[Enrollment]
Total enrollment: 571 (2020)

[Description]
The Warsaw University of Technology Business School was established in 1991 in a joint initiative with the Warsaw University of Technology, London Business School, Norwegian School of Economics and HEC Paris. The MBA program was one of the first MBA programs in Poland, launched in 1992.

The MBA programs are interwoven with technological studies and innovation. "This immersion," says Dr. Grazyna Rembielak, director of the Quality and Development Department, "is written into the DNA of the Warsaw University of Technology." Students can take an Executive MBA or choose the MBA program with one of three specializations: Digital Transformation, Finance and Technology, or Kaizen Industry 4.0. What is unique about the methods of the school, says Grazyna, is the focus placed on "experiential learning through practice." Students are also expected to learn to empathize and understand themselves and their partners, acquiring the soft skills needed in leadership. As opposed to the traditional one-way transfer of knowledge from the lecturer to students, the classes are based on the notion of cocreation and the *exchange of knowledge* between the lecturer and the students, and also between the students themselves.

The Executive MBA program is the school's flagship program and is based on a three pillars approach: Knowledge for Business (aiming to consolidate and systemize knowledge), Business in Action (putting the acquired knowledge into practice) and Personal Development: Transformation Labs (highlighting the strength of the students and potential development areas). Another notable program offered at the school is Total Design Management, created and run in cooperation with the Institute of Industrial Design. This program deals with business and design, paying particular attention to the benefits of innovation within the Polish market. The structure of the program is based mainly on workshops that allow students to acquire design manager competencies.

[Apply to]
business.edu.pl or mba.rekrutacja@biznes.edu.pl

[Links]
Web: **business.edu.pl** LinkedIn: **school/wutbs** Facebook: **szkolabiznesupw**
Instagram: **@szkolabiznesupw**

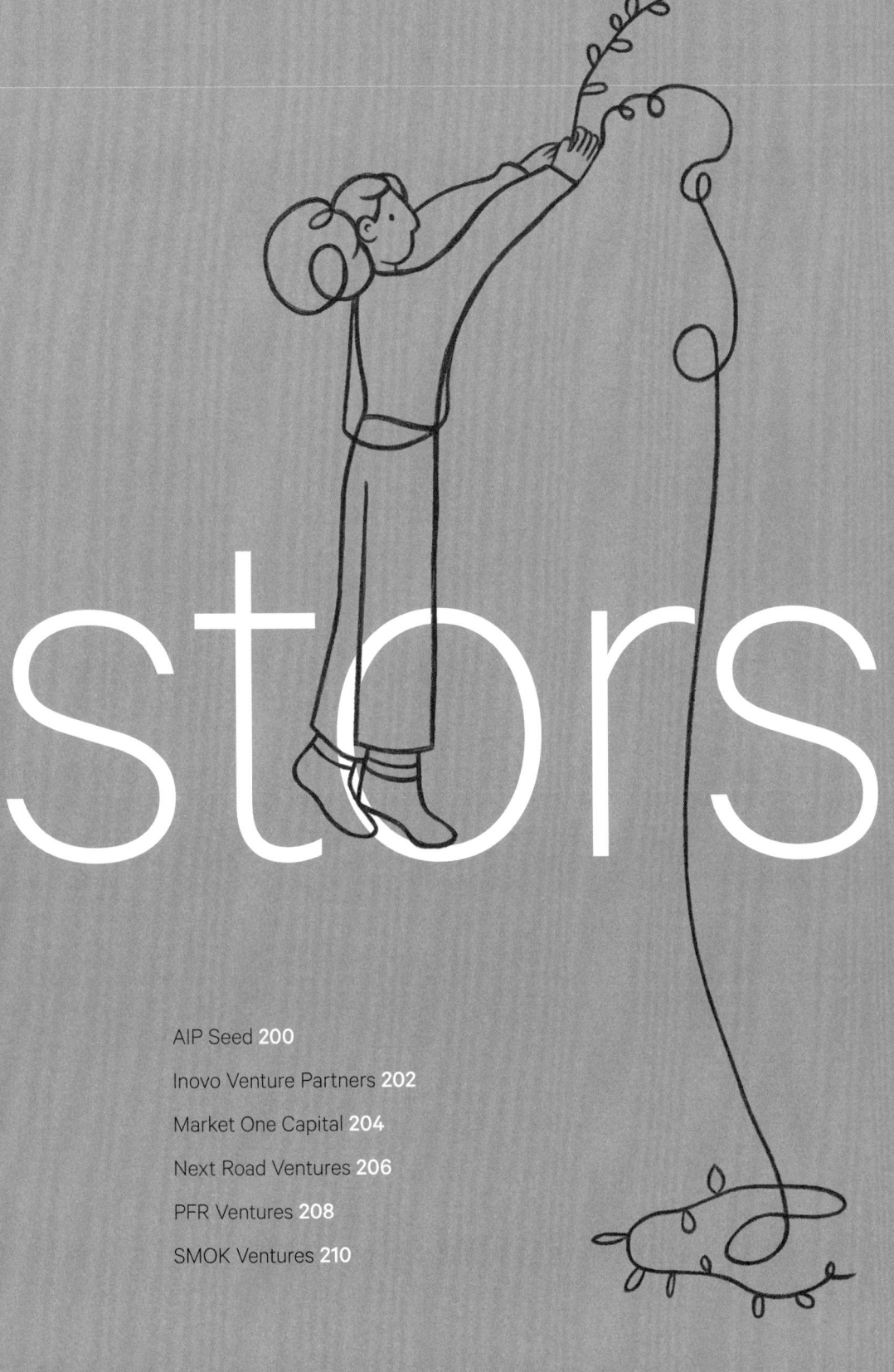

stors

- **Set clear goals.**
  This one is key for us. Approach the investment round like a project and show us that your team can set and achieve stretch goals.

- **Be ambitious.**
  Show us that you have a growth-oriented model and that you want to build a billion-dollar business.

- **Build a founding team.**
  Growth-focused founders need many skills, and we want to see that you can build and lead a team.

- **Show traction or interest.**
  We want to see that you have built something, however small, and that you have been able to generate some income from your core idea or at least can prove demand.

- **Have a big idea.**
  We're looking for ideas that are disruptive, unique and competitive and that have the potential to change up their industry.

[Name] # AIP Seed

[Elevator Pitch] *"Our goal is to be the first investor in top CEE startups. We want to promote innovation and progress in the regional startup ecosystem by providing early-stage founders with smart capital, closing the gap between incubation and seed-round stages."*

[Sector] **Disruptive technology**

[Description] AIP Seed was founded in 2011 to create an ecosystem in which entrepreneurs could fulfill their goals, a mission still pursued by the fund's CEO, Dariusz Zuk. AIP Seed invests up to €100,000 ($119,000) in early-stage startups based in the CEE region. This strategy stems from the fund's mission but also reflects a specific investment thesis: AIP Seed believes that early seed has a favorable risk-reward profile compared to later stages. AIP Seed leans towards disruptive ideas that add positive value to their sector. One of its early investments, Glov, is a makeup remover that uses microfiber technology to remove makeup using only the addition of water. Since launching in 2012, Glov has expanded to most major markets and has received awards such as Allure's The Beauty Expert in 2015 and EY's Entrepreneur of the Year in 2016. In 2020, AIP Seed invested in Plenti, an on-demand electronics rental platform offering new or nearly new devices such as VR headsets, robot vacuums and drones to enable access without ownership. And its most recent investment, Foodsi, combats food waste through a marketplace for surplus meals.

AIP Seed connects with potential investments through several channels: website inquiries are always open, it maintains a strong network of business partners and other investors who refer promising entrepreneurs, and it interacts with the ecosystem via pitching events and browsing LinkedIn for any promising leads. Once invested, AIP Seed forms close relationships with the startup teams, providing support in further fundraising, corporate partnerships, international expansion and mergers and acquisitions. Associates also assist with more hands-on problem solving, using their own expertise or reaching out to AIP Seed's network. "We don't cheer from the sidelines," says Boris Kocot, Investment Associate. "Instead, we look to add value to these fantastic companies, and it is an ever-developing relationship."

[Apply to] aipseed.com

[Links] Web: aipseed.com LinkedIn: company/aip-seed Facebook: AIP-Seed-530251990773881

- **Be an ambitious startup in Poland or the CEE region.**
  We invest in startups and founders in Poland and all over CEE.

- **Be an early-stage tech company.**
  We invest mainly in the seed stage (occasionally earlier or later). Our initial ticket is €0.5 million to €3 million and we have reserved budgets for follow-up investments.

- **Be a "moonshot" company.**
  We partner with companies that attack large markets: startups that can reach $100 million revenue in the next five to seven years and become unicorns and eventually decacorns.

- **Offer products that significantly improve clients' lives.**
  We are looking for products that significantly improve clients' lives, whether that's through cutting-edge technology or an outstanding user experience.

Inovo Venture Partners

[Name]

[Elevator Pitch] *"We are a venture capital fund investing between €0.5 million and €3 million in rapidly growing early-stage tech companies across Poland and CEE."*

[Sector] **Technology**

[Description] Inovo Venture Partners is a first-choice VC for ambitious founders from Poland and the CEE region. It backs early-stage, post-traction startups with up to €3 million ($3.5 million) of initial investment and helps them to build global brands while also driving growth to the local startup ecosystem. It strives to be the best early-stage fund in Poland and the CEE region and to be in direct competition with, or a better option than, tier-one US funds for Polish and CEE founders. Some of its portfolio companies include Booksy, Spacelift, Zowie, Tidio, Jutro Medical and Infermedica.

Tomasz Swieboda, CEO and managing partner at Inovo, had previously worked at various financial institutions, but it was only when he started angel investing that he realized the great potential in early Polish entrepreneurs and startups and technology companies. His background in entrepreneurship had shown him just how difficult it was to run a business but also how possible it was to support entrepreneurs and projects with the potential to become very large internationally. Tomasz and the rest of the team, including Michal Rokosz and Maciej Malysz, support CEE-originated companies in becoming global leaders in their markets and encourage founders and employees to contribute further to the ecosystem. They plan to fundamentally change the Polish investment ecosystem by continuing to take on ambitious projects.

In addition to its partners' expertise, Inovo also provides all of the resources a founder and company needs to succeed at every stage in their growth, even matching founders with international advisors. Inovo also has a full-time recruiter on board who helps business owners choose the right people for their prospective team, and the firm co-invests with other supportive partners to maximize the success of the brands in its portfolio.

[Apply to] pitch@inovo.vc

[Links] Web: inovo.vc LinkedIn: company/i18s Facebook: inovovc

- **Be concise.**
  We want a to-the-point pitch deck with a logical flow of information.

- **Be clear.**
  Present a credible value proposition.

- **Present a differentiated product.**
  Present an in-depth analysis of the market for G2 Marketing Solutions.

- **Have great storytelling skills.**
  Show us that you have the ability to attract great talent and individual investors who are industry insiders.

- **Have supportive investors.**
  For us to partner with you, it is crucial for you to have supportive investors who trust you and give you total freedom in the decision-making process.

[Name] # Market One Capital

[Elevator Pitch] *"We want you to understand best when, where and in what we invest."*

[Sector] **Digital platforms**

[Description] Market One Capital connects new businesses to experts and mentors and builds the needed investment syndicates in follow-on rounds. It provides investment as well as aid and deep expertise to Europe-based digital platforms or marketplace business, whether B2C or B2B, at the pre-seed or seed stage. It believes that a successful venture relies on a profound knowledge of why you are in this business and what your role is in it.

Marcin Kurek, the managing partner, has been in the tech industry for seventeen years, during which time he worked for one startup, founded another, became an angel investor and finally became a general partner. He became an active investor in 2012 and met Marcin Zabielski. After years of successful cooperation, they decided to make use of their backgrounds and expertise to create their "ideal" venture fund. In 2018, they launched Market One Capital, a venture firm with the exact characteristics they hoped for. They made it a seed fund, as this is where they could bring the most value. Market One Capital's funds go to areas in which they have the most experience, such as digital platforms and marketplaces. They aim to provide support for talents all over Europe, with a special focus on CEE.

Market One Capital became the first VC of Polish origins to invest in a unicorn company at an early stage. It provided support for TIER Mobility, a shared micro-mobility provider, in 2019. With a $2 billion valuation, TIER has raised a total of $660 million in equity and debt funding to date. It also invested in instant-grocery-delivery startup JORK at seed stage. It earned an overall valuation of $1.2 billion in just 7 months. Currently, Market One Capital receives eight thousand projects annually to review and analyze, which amounts to about twenty-five to thirty projects a day.

[Apply to] moc.vc

[Links] Web: moc.vc LinkedIn: company/m1c Facebook: marketonecapital
Twitter: @Market1Capital

- **Be ambitious.**
  We strive to invest in founders that aim to build a potential global leader.

- **Research the market size.**
  We need to see that early revenues are present and that there is a potential for the startup to deliver outsized returns.

- **Know your competitive advantage.**
  Does your company offer a solution that is unique or substantially better than what is currently available? Make sure to outline your points of parity.

- **Show us your unique insight.**
  It's important for us that the founders and team have the right qualities, business, and technical ability, and some unique insights into the market to make the project a success. So make sure to show us what makes you stand out.

[Name]

Next Road Ventures

[Elevator Pitch]

"We are an early-stage venture capital fund investing in European companies at their seed rounds. We also support portfolio companies with the necessary network, expertise, resources and funds to help them grow and expand."

[Sector]

Multiple

[Description]

Next Road Ventures is a VC investment firm that is based in Warsaw and invests in the early stages of companies based throughout Europe. Backed by a global network of business angels and Vestbee, the leading matchmaking platform for startups, as well as accelerators, VC funds and corporates, Next Road Ventures not only supports its portfolio companies with funding but also with expertise, resources, business support, free tools and an international network.

While it describes itself as industry agnostic, it does have a preference for companies operating in ICT (information and communications technology), big data, SaaS, fintech, Industry 4.0 and technology sectors across Europe, with an emphasis on CEE. "Our sweet spot," says Marcin Laczynski, cofounder and partner at Next Road Ventures, "are companies looking to raise up to one million euros in pre-seed and seed stages." Its initial ticket size is generally €250,000 ($295,000) with a potential top up of €750,000 ($885,000). "Today, our portfolio consists of companies established by founders of different backgrounds and geographies." Some of the notable startups supported by Next Road Ventures include SunRoof.se, a solar roof company; Smabbler, a deep text understanding engine; and Amberlo, a law-practice management software.

The firm was founded in 2019 by Marcin and his close friend, Ewa Chronowska, cofounder and partner at Next Road Ventures. Ewa and Marcin are two die-hard entrepreneurs and startup enthusiasts (both with over fifteen years of experience) who have known each other since high school. Ewa has a background in consulting, corporate finance and investment while Marcin's background is in small and medium enterprises (SME) internationalization in Europe and Asia. "We firmly believe that the right people can disrupt any industry," says Marcin. Due to this belief, the two search for committed entrepreneurs with scalable business who are willing to go the extra mile to build global businesses.

[Apply to]

nextroad.vc or office@nextroad.vc

[Links]

Web: **nextroad.vc** LinkedIn: **company/nextroadventures** Facebook: **nextroadventures**

- **Check the fund strategy.**
  Most of our funds are agnostic in the case of the sector but may have preferences in terms of ticket size and business model.

- **Make your own due diligence.**
  Check the fund portfolio and speak to the founders they've supported to make sure they're the right fit.

- **Be ready for the results.**
  Be aware that venture capital funds are focused on profit and they will push your company to develop fast.

- **Check the startup.pfr.pl website**
  There are plenty of interviews with fund managers in which they share their investment criteria.

[Name] # PFR Ventures

[Elevator Pitch] *"We are an institutional investor focused on venture capital and private equity funds. We create and manage deployment programs to invest in local and international management teams."*

[Sector] **Multiple**

[Description] PFR Ventures, the largest fund investor in the CEE region, strives to support both innovative small and medium Polish enterprises at any stage of their development via venture capital funds, and mature companies via private equity funds. Within its portfolio, it currently has more than fifty available funds, which have made a total of four hundred investments to date. As a fund of fund managers, PFR Ventures, together with private investors, angel investors and corporations, invests in venture capital and private equity funds. This means that while it does not invest directly in companies, interested entrepreneurs can research and find funds within the PFR Ventures portfolio that will meet their needs. Entrepreneurs can select between private equity, venture capital, business angels and corporate venture capital funds.

While the investment size varies between funds, they range between less than 1 million zł ($262,000) and more than 25 million zł ($6.5 million). Entrepreneurs can also apply filters including "fund status" and "industries" to aid in their search for the appropriate fund. The sectors currently being supported include, but are not limited to, artificial intelligence, agritech, 3D printing, healthcare, software, pharmaceuticals, travel and quantum computing. Once the appropriate fund is found, entrepreneurs can use the PFR Ventures website to directly contact the chosen fund.

Among the most notable startups supported by PFR Ventures are Booksy, a booking application for beauty businesses; and iTaxi, a free mobile application that allows its users to order cabs through its application. With the CEE region becoming Europe's fastest emerging startup ecosystem and Poland being the region's largest economy, there is no better time than the present for innovative startups to receive the support they need.

[Apply to] kontakt@pfrventures.pl or pfrventures.pl

[Links] Web: **pfrventures.pl** LinkedIn: **company/pfr-ventures** Facebook: **PFRInnowacje** Twitter: **@PFRInnowacje**

- **Check our website.**
  We provide you with as much information as we can on our website, including an extensive FAQ page. Read all the information carefully before you reach out.

- **Prove your leadership.**
  We're looking for serial entrepreneurs who can show us a history of success and, of course, many failures. Show us that you've done this before, and we take it as a sign that you can do it again.

- **Show us your traction.**
  If you're a first-time founder, show us what you've done with your company so far. Additionally, we'd like to get to know you more before making a call. Attending ReaktorX, our acceleration program, is a good way to introduce yourself.

- **Have a deep understanding of your industry.**
  Be the person that others go to when they need an expert. We require an in-depth knowledge of the industry from all our founders.

[Name]
SMOK Ventures

[Elevator Pitch] *"We are a Polish-American venture capital firm that invests in early-stage CEE startups, in the software and game-development sector."*

[Sector] **Software and game development**

[Description] In 2015, current SMOK Ventures managing partner Borys Musielak was selling his previous startup Filmaster to Samba TV. While in the US, he met Paul Bragiel, an American angel investor and venture capitalist who had previously invested in companies like Uber and Stripe. So, when deciding to cofound SMOK Ventures in Poland with Diana Koziarska, with whom he had previously cofounded an acceleration program, Borys reached out to Paul, who became the third managing partner at SMOK.

SMOK Ventures is a Polish-American venture capital firm that typically invests between $50,000 to $1 million in the very early stages of startups in CEE. However, while its main focus is the software and game-development sector, it does not limit itself to specific industries. SMOK's prime targets are top founders with proven track records. This is what allows it to identify and receive top projects from serial founders and to invest in their projects even as early as the pre-revenue stage. But it does not shy away from investing into first-time founders with product traction or useful experience. Some of the notable startups in SMOK's portfolio include SunRoof, a solar roof company; ProperGate, a smart delivery-management system that provides real-time information of materials on complex construction sites; and Rezuro, a click-to-rent platform for tenants and landlords.

What makes SMOK stand out in the market is that it's not only a highly diverse and international team but also a firm ready to invest in something crazy. It thinks big and expects its founders to think globally as well. Currently, the SMOK Ventures team is working on developing its second fund, which is expected to be five times bigger than SMOK 1.

[Apply to] smok@smok.vc

[Links] Web: **smok.vc** LinkedIn: **company/smok-ventures** Facebook: **Smokventures** Twitter: **@smokvc**

" *CES offers two main areas of business support: access to its coworking space at preferential rates, and a One-Stop Store for businesses that provides a wealth of information.* "

Startup Support / Center of Entrepreneurship Smolna (CES)

[Elevator Pitch] *"Since 2013, we've been supporting entrepreneurs and SMEs to kickstart and develop their businesses through our unparalleled program of incubation, information and our broad range of free services and tools."*

[Sector] Multiple

Established in 2013, the Center of Entrepreneurship Smolna (CES) is situated in the heart of Warsaw yet surrounded by greenery and with great access to the Warszawa-Powiśle railway station. CES offers hands-on and practical tools and resources to early-stage businesses and entrepreneurs.

CES offers two main areas of business support: access to its coworking space at preferential rates, and a One-Stop Store for businesses that provides a wealth of information. CES's coworking space comprises forty desks and two conference rooms, and eligible startups can rent the desks at a discounted rate. Individuals and organizations that are registered in Poland and have been trading for less than three years are eligible to apply. Through CES's One Stop Store, startups can register and incorporate their business and receive information on events and programs for entrepreneurs in Warsaw as well as on EU loans and subsidies for setting up and developing a business. The One Stop Store provides participants with a hub of curated information and tailored support.

Through regular events, newsletters and partner visits, CES offers unrivaled access to the local entrepreneurial and commercial ecosystem. Its large and extended network encompasses local and global partners from both the private and public sectors. CES provides many opportunities for startups to collaborate with its partners and guides them as to how they can build mutually beneficial relationships. CES also runs regular internationalization programs to help Warsaw startups scale up. The most recent ones were Startup Woche Dusseldorf (three days) and Digital Demo Day (two days), which were both run in Dusseldorf, Germany, but these will expand to other EU locations in the future. Study visits to business hubs and incubators are also frequently organized by CES, offering local high school students the chance to find out more about entrepreneurial topics.

[Links] Web: biznes.um.warszawa.pl LinkedIn: showcase/grow-with-warsaw
Facebook: CentrumPrzedsiebiorczosciSmolna

directory

The following selection is a brief choice of organizations, companies and contacts available in Warsaw

Startups

Apollo
Planteris Spółka z o.o.
ul. Racjonalizacji 5
02-673 Warsaw
apollo.store

Authologic
ul. Sklepowa 24
02-482 Warsaw
authologic.com

EcoBean
Koszykowa 75
00-662 Warsaw
ecobean.pl

Jutro Medical
ul. Powązkowska 44
01-797 Warsaw
jutromedical.com/en

LogicAI
logicai.com

Packhelp
ul. Kolejowa 5/7
01-217 Warsaw
packhelp.com

Planet Heroes
planetheroes.app

ProperGate
Targowa 56
03-733 Warsaw
propergate.co

Skriware
ul. Kolejowa 19/21
01-217 Warsaw
skriware.com

Vue Storefront
ul. Prosta 20
00-850 Warsaw
vuestorefront.io

Programs

Akademickie Inkubatory Przedsiębiorczości (AIP)
Al. Poniatowskiego 1
03-901 Warsaw
aip.link

Foodtech.ac
HubHub Nowogrodzka Square
al. Jerozolimskie 93
02-001 Warsaw
foodtech.ac

Foundation for Technology Entrepreneurship, MIT Enterprise Forum CEE
HubHub Nowogrodzka Square
al. Jerozolimskie 93
02-001 Warsaw
mitefcee.org

Google for Startups Campus
Centrum Praskie Koneser
pl. Konesera 10
03-736 Warsaw
campus.co/warsaw/programs

Microsoft For Startups
al. Jerozolimskie 195A
02-222 Warsaw
startups.microsoft.com

NEXT Acceleration Program For Female Founders
Fundacja Przedsiębiorczości Kobiet
Female Entrepreneurship Foundation
ul. Konstruktorska 11
02-673 Warsaw
siecprzedsiebiorczychkobiet.pl

PFR School of Pioneers
Polish Development Fund
ul. Krucza 50
00-025 Warsaw
startup.pfr.pl/en/
pfr-school-pioneers

ReaktorX
ul. Franciszka Bohomolca 15
01-638 Warsaw
reaktorx.com

Startup Hub Poland
WORKIN
Senatorska 2
00-075 Warsaw
startuphub.pl

Warsaw Booster
warsawbooster21.pl

Spaces

The Brain Embassy
Adgar Park West
al. Jerozolimskie 181B
Warsaw 02-222
brainembassy.com

Centrum Kreatywności Targowa
ul. Targowa 56
03-733 Warszawa
cktargowa.pl

CIC Warsaw
Varso Place
Chmielna 73
00-801 Warsaw
cic.com/warsaw

District Hall
Varso Place
ul. Chmielna 73
00-801 Warsaw
venturecafewarsaw.org

Google for Startups Campus
Centrum Praskie Koneser
pl. Konesera 10
03-736 Warsaw
campus.co/warsaw

HubHub
al. Jerozolimskie 93
02-001 Warsaw
hubhub.com/en/warsaw
-nowogrodzka-square

Mindspace Koszyki
ul. Koszykowa 61 and 65
00-667 Warsaw
mindspace.me

Some of the websites in the Directory require the 'www' prefix.

WeWork
Grzybowska 60
00-844 Warsaw
wework.com/l/office-space/
warsaw

Experts

EIT InnoEnergy Central
Europe
ul. Wielicka 28
30-552 Krakow
innoenergy.com

Google for Startups Campus
Centrum Praskie Koneser
pl. Konesera 10
03-736 Warsaw
campus.co/warsaw

Santander Bank Polska SA
al. Jana Pawła II 17
00-854 Warsaw
santander.pl

Venture Cafe Warsaw
Foundation
Chmielna 73
00-801 Warsaw
venturecafewarsaw.org

Visa Europe Management
Services Limited
Oddział w Polsce
Bud. Varso 2
Chmielna 73
00-801 Warsaw
visa.pl

Founders

Audioteka
ul. Konstruktorska 12
02-673 Warsaw
audioteka.com

Digital University
ul. Krakowskie Przedmieście 13
00-071 Warsaw
digitaluniversity.pl

Dronehub
CIC Warsaw
ul. Chmielna 73
00-801 Warsaw
dronehub.ai

Prowly
ul. Antoniego Józefa
Madalińskiego 71/1
02-549 Warsaw
prowly.com

Telemedi
ul. Marynarska 13
02-674 Warsaw
telemedi.com

Schools

Kozminski University
Jagiellońska 57/59
03-301 Warsaw
kozminski.edu.pl

SGH Warsaw School
of Economics
al. Niepodległości 162
02-554 Warsaw
sgh.waw.pl

University of Warsaw
Faculty of Management
ul. Szturmowa 1/3
02-678 Warsaw
wz.uw.edu.pl/en

Warsaw University of
Technology Business School
ul. Koszykowa 79
02-008 Warsaw
business.edu.pl

Investors

AIP Seed
al. Księcia Józefa
Poniatowskiego 1
03-901 Warsaw
aipseed.com

Inovo Venture Partners
HubHub Nowogrodzka Square
al. Jerozolimskie 93
02-001 Warsaw
inovo.vc

Market One Capital
ul. Widok 16/1
00-023 Warsaw
moc.vc

Next Road Ventures
ul. Padewska 23/7
00-777 Warsaw
nextroad.vc

PFR Ventures
Krucza 50
00-025 Warsaw
pfrventures.pl

SMOK Ventures
smok.vc

Startup Support

Center of Entrepreneurship
Smolna (CES)
Biuro Rozwoju Gospodarczego
Ul. Smolna 4
00-375 Warsaw
biznes.um.warszawa.pl

Accommodation

domiporta
domiporta.pl

Foreigners Warsaw / Flats /
Accommodation
facebook.com/
groups/571354199689387

otodom
otodom.pl

Banks

Alior Bank
aliorbank.pl/en

Bank Pekao S.A
pekao.com.pl

BOŚ Bank
bosbank.pl/en

Citi Handlowy
citibank.pl/en

ING Bank Śląski
ing.pl

mBank
mbank.pl

Millenium bank
bankmillennium.pl/en

PNB Paribas
bnpparibas.pl/en/english-info

PKO Bank Polski
pkobp.pl

Santander Bank Polska
santander.pl/en

Coffee Shops and Places with Wifi

Café Bristol
Krakowskie Przedmieście 42/44
Warsaw 00-325
cafebristol.pl

Cafe Kafka
Oboźna 3
00-340 Warsaw
kawiarnia-kafka.pl

Coffee Desk
Wilcza 42
Warsaw
kawiarnia.coffeedesk.pl/#koncepcja-kawiarni

Coffee Karma
Mokotowska 17
00-640 Warsaw
coffeekarma.eu

Costa Coffee
(various locations)
costacoffee.pl

Etno Café
(various locations)
etnocafe.pl/en/coffee-shops

E. Wedel Chocolate Café
wedelpijalnie.pl/lokale#lista-pijalni

Francuska 30
Francuska 30
03-905 Warsaw
facebook.com/francuska.trzydziesci

Green Caffe Nero
(various locations)
greencaffenero.pl/en

Ministerstwo Kawy
Marszałkowska 27/35
00-639 Warsaw
facebook.com/MinisterstwoKawy

Starbucks
(various locations)
en.starbucks.pl

STOR Café
Tamka 33
Warsaw
stor.cafe

To Lubię
Freta 8
00-227 Warsaw
tolubie.pl

Financial Services

EY
ey.com/pl_pl

Deloitte Warsaw
al. Jana Pawła II 22
00-133 Warsaw
deloitte.com

KPMG Poland
Inflancka 4a
00-189 Warsaw
home.kpmg/pl/en

Groups and Meetups

ExpatHelp
expathelp.pl

Expats in Warsaw
facebook.com/groups/750111925124070

InterNations - Warsaw Expats
internations.org/warsaw-expats

Meetup - Expats in Warsaw
meetup.com/Expats-in-Warsaw

Important Government Offices

City Hall of Warsaw
Bankowy Square 3/5
00-950 Warsaw
en.um.warszawa.pl

Ministry of Foreign Affairs
al. J. Ch. Szucha 23
00-580 Warsaw
gov.pl/web/dyplomacja

Office for Foreigners
ul. Koszykowa 16
00-564 Warsaw
gov.pl/web/udsc

Polish Chamber of Commerce
ul. Trębacka 4
00-074 Warsaw
kig.pl

Smolna 38
Smolna 38
00-375 Warsaw
smolna38.com/en

Warsaw Tourist Office
Palace of Culture and Science,
plac Defilad 1
00-901 Warsaw
warsawtour.pl/en/main-page

Insurance Companies

Allianz
allianz.pl

AVIVA
aviva.pl

AXA
axa-assistance.pl

Generali
generali.pl

InterRisk
interrisk.pl

LINK4
link4.pl

Prudential
prudential.pl

PZU
pzu.pl/en

Warta
warta.pl

Language Schools

**Edu & More Sp. z o. o. -
Polish Language School
for Foreigners**
44 Nowogrodzka Str.,
intercom 7
00-695 Warsaw
polishonlinenow.com/en

**IKO – Polish Language School
for Foreigners**
ul. Foksal 16
00-372 Warsaw
iko.com.pl

Klub Dialogu
55 Aleje Jerozolimskie St, flat 4
00-697 Warsaw
klubdialogu.pl

Lingua Polonica
Filtrowa 59/lok.25
02-056 Warsaw
linguapolonica.com.pl/en

**Polski Instytut Językowy -
Polish Linguistic Institute**
Mazowiecka 12/24
00-048 Warsaw
instytutjezykowy.pl/en

ProfiLingua
profi-lingua.pl/szkola
-jezykowa/warszawa

Legal

CMS
Warsaw Financial Centre
ul. Emilii Plater 53
00-113 Warsaw
cms.law/en/pol

**Dowlegal Adwokaci
Decowska-Olejnik sp. K.**
ul. Wspólna 50A lok. 22
00-684 Warsaw
dowlegal.pl/en

Law More
ul. Dzielna 60 (klatka J)
01-029 Warsaw
lawmore.pl

Wardyński & Partners
al. Ujazdowskie 10
00-478 Warsaw
wardynski.com.pl/en

Startup Events

Aula Polska
facebook.com/aula.polska

Founder Institute Warsaw
fi.co/events/warsaw

Geek Girls Carrots
facebook.com/ggcarrots

IT events
crossweb.pl/wydarzenia

Startup Grind Warsaw
startupgrind.com/warsaw

**Venture Café
Thursday Gathering**
venturecafewarsaw.org/
programs/thursday-gathering

Wolves Summit
wolvessummit.com

glossary

A

accelerator — an organization or program that offers advice and resources to help small businesses grow

acqui-hire — the process of buying out a company based on the skills of its staff rather than its service or product

AI (artificial intelligence) — the simulation of human intelligence by computer systems; machines that are able to perform tasks normally carried out by humans

angel investment — outside funding with shared ownership equity typically made possible by an affluent individual who provides a startup with starting capital

[see also: **business angel**]

API (application programming interface) — an interface or communication protocol between a client and a server that simplifies the building of client-side software

ARR (accounting or average rate of return) — the calculation generated from net income of the proposed capital investment

B

B2B (business-to-business) — the exchange of services, information and/or products from a business to a business

B2C (business-to-consumer) — the exchange of services, information and/or products from a business to a consumer

B Corporation — a certification issued to for-profit companies by the nonprofit B Lab, which certifies that businesses meet standards of social and environmental performance, accountability and transparency

blockchain — a digital, public collection of financial accounts in which transactions made in bitcoin or another cryptocurrency are recorded chronologically

BOM (bill of materials) — a list of the parts or components required to build a product

bootstrapping — to self-fund, without outside investment

bridge loan — a loan taken out for a short-term period, typically between two weeks and three years, until long-term financing can be organized

burn rate — the amount of money a startup spends

business angel — an experienced entrepreneur or professional who provides starting or growth capital for promising startups

[see also: angel investment]

business model canvas — a template that offers a coherent overview of the key drivers of a business in order to bring innovation into current or new business models

C

C-level — a corporate title given to high-ranking executives responsible for making company-wide decisions

CAC (customer acquisition cost) — the amount needed to pay in marketing and sales in order to acquire one user

cap table — an analysis of ownership stakes in a company

carbon dioxide equivalent (CO_2eq) — a unit of greenhouse gas that has the equivalent global warming potential (GWP) as one metric tonne of CO_2. Essentially a measurement of environmental impact.

CEE — Central and Eastern Europe

CEO (chief executive officer) — the highest-ranking person in a company, responsible for taking on managerial decisions

circular economy — an economic system aimed at eliminating waste by sharing, leasing, reusing, repairing, refurbishing and recycling existing materials and products for as long as possible

CMO (chief marketing officer) — a corporate executive responsible for marketing activities in an organization or company

cold-calling — the solicitation of potential customers who had no prior interaction with the solicitor

convertible note/bond — a type of short-term debt often used by seed investors to delay establishing a valuation for the startup until a later round of funding or milestone

COO (chief operating officer) — a high-level executive running the operations of a company

coworking space — A shared working environment

CPA (cost per action or acquisition) — the average cost for a conversion from one's advertising campaign

CPC (cost per click) — an internet advertising model used to drive traffic to websites in which an advertiser pays a publisher when the ad is clicked

D

dealflow — a term for investors that refers to the rate at which they receive potential business deals

diluting — a reduction in the ownership percentage of a share of stock due to new equity shares being issued

E

early-stage — the stage in which financing is provided by a venture capital firm to a company after the seed round; a company stage in which a product or service is still in development but not on the market yet

elevator pitch — a short description of an idea, product or company that explains the concept

exit — a way to transition the ownership of a company to another company

F

fintech — financial technology; a technology or innovation that aims to compete with traditional financial methods in the delivery of financial services

flex desk — a shared desk available for temporary use in a coworking space

I

incubator — a facility established to nurture young startup firms during their first few months or years of development

installed base — the number of units of a product that have been sold and are actually being used

IP (intellectual property) — property which is not tangible; the result of creativity, such as ideas that can be patented and protected by copyright

IPO (initial public offering) — the first time a company's stock is offered for sale to the public

K

KPI (key performance indicator) — value that is measurable and demonstrates how effectively a company is achieving its key business objectives

L

later-stage — the stage in which companies have typically demonstrated viability as a going concern and have a product with a strong market presence

lean — lean startup methodology; the method proposed by Eric Ries in his book on developing businesses and startups through product-development cycles

Lean LaunchPad — a methodology for entrepreneurs to test and develop business models based on inquiring with and learning from customers

M

M&A (mergers and acquisitions) — a merger is a process by which two companies join to form a new company, while an acquisition is the purchase of one company by another where no new company is formed

martech — marketing technology

MAU (monthly active users) — a performance metric for the success of an internet product

MVP (minimum viable product) — a product with just enough features to satisfy early customers who can provide feedback for future product development

O

opportunity fund — an investment vehicle in companies or sectors in areas where growth opportunities are anticipated

P

pitch — an opportunity to introduce a business idea in a limited amount of time to potential investors, often using a presentation

pitch deck — a shorter version of a business plan that presents key figures generally to investors

pivot — the process when a company quickly changes direction after previously targeting a different market segment

proof of concept (POC) — a test conducted for the purpose of showing potential investors, managers and other stakeholders that an idea of a startup has tangible financial viability and promise and can be taken to the commercialization stage

PR kit (press release kit or press kit) — a package of promotional materials, such as pictures, logos and descriptions of a company

product-market fit — a product that has created significant customer value and its best target industries have been identified

pro-market — a market or capitalist economy

S

SaaS (software as a service) — a software distribution model in which a third-party provider hosts applications and makes them available to customers

scaleup — a company that has already validated its product in a market and is economically sustainable

SDGs (sustainable development goals) — a United Nations agenda that covers seventeen global goals that can be achieved by reaching 169 defined targets

SDG indicators — an indication used to measure the progress in reaching the Sustainable Development Goals

[see also: **UN Goals for Sustainable Development and sustainable development**]

seed funding — the first round of venture capital funding (typically called the seed round); a small, early-stage investment from family members, friends, banks or an investor, also known as a seed investor

series A/B/C/D — the subsequent funding rounds that come after the seed stage and aim to raise further capital (up to $1 million) when the company demonstrates various increase factors

shares — a unit of ownership of a company that belong to a shareholder

SME — small to medium enterprise

social entrepreneur — a person who establishes an enterprise with the aim of solving social problems and/or effecting social change

social impact investing — investment that brings together capital and expertise from the public, private and not-for-profit sectors to achieve a social objective

solopreneurs — a person who sets up and runs a business on their own and typically does not hire employees

startup — companies under three years old that are in the growth stage and starting to become profitable (if not already)

STEAM — science, technology, engineering, arts and math

sustainable development — defined by the UN World Commission on Environment and Development as an organizing principle that "meets the needs of the present without compromising the ability of future generations to meet their own needs."

SVP (senior vice president) — an officer of an organization who reports to the president or CEO and functions as the second in command in rank within the company

T

term sheet/letter of intent — a document between an investor and a startup including the conditions for financing (commonly nonbinding)

U

unicorn — a company, often in the tech or software sector, worth over US$1 billion

UN Goals for Sustainable Development (SDG) — Seventeen intergovernmental development goals established by all 193 members of the United Nations in 2015 for the year 2030. The SDGs' non-binding targets provide a framework for organizations and businesses to think about and begin addressing the world's most important challenges

[see also: **SDGs and sustainable development**]

USP (unique selling point) — a factor that differentiates a product from its competitors

UX (user experience design) — the process of designing and improving user satisfaction with products so that they are useful, easy to use and pleasurable to interact with

V

valuation — the amount of money a company is worth; typically happens at every stage of funding

VC (venture capital) — a form of financing that comes from a pool of investors in a venture capital firm in return for equity

vesting — a process that involves giving or earning a right to a present or future payment, benefit or asset

Z

zebra — a company that aims for sustainable prosperity and is powered by people who work together to create change beyond a positive financial return

STARTUP GUIDE JOHANNESBURG — The Entrepreneur's Handbook
STARTUP GUIDE HAMBURG — The Entrepreneur's Handbook
STARTUP GUIDE AMSTERDAM — The Entrepreneur's Handbook
STARTUP GUIDE CAPE TOWN — The Entrepreneur's Handbook
STARTUP GUIDE LUXEMBOURG — The Entrepreneur's Handbook
STARTUP GUIDE VIENNA — The Entrepreneur's Handbook
STARTUP GUIDE TEL AVIV — The Entrepreneur's Handbook
STARTUP GUIDE MADRID — The Entrepreneur's Handbook
STARTUP GUIDE COPENHAGEN — The Entrepreneur's Handbook
IMPACT GUIDE SERIES STARTUP GUIDE JAPAN — The Entrepreneur's Handbook
STARTUP GUIDE PARIS — The Entrepreneur's Handbook
STARTUP GUIDE LOS ANGELES — The Entrepreneur's Handbook
STARTUP GUIDE REYKJAVIK — The Entrepreneur's Handbook
STARTUP GUIDE STOCKHOLM — The Entrepreneur's Handbook
STARTUP GUIDE MUNICH — The Entrepreneur's Handbook
STARTUP GUIDE FRANKFURT — The Entrepreneur's Handbook
STARTUP GUIDE ZURICH — The Entrepreneur's Handbook
STARTUP GUIDE LONDON — The Entrepreneur's Handbook
STARTUP GUIDE TOKYO — The Entrepreneur's Handbook
STARTUP GUIDE LISBON — The Entrepreneur's Handbook
IMPACT GUIDE SERIES STARTUP GUIDE SWITZERLAND — The Entrepreneur's Handbook
STARTUP GUIDE SINGAPORE — The Entrepreneur's Handbook
STARTUP GUIDE NEW YORK — The Entrepreneur's Handbook
IMPACT GUIDE SERIES STARTUP GUIDE EGYPT — The Entrepreneur's Handbook
STARTUP GUIDE BANGKOK — The Entrepreneur's Handbook
STARTUP GUIDE BERLIN — The Entrepreneur's Handbook
IMPACT GUIDE SERIES STARTUP GUIDE LAGOS — The Entrepreneur's Handbook
IMPACT GUIDE SERIES STARTUP GUIDE ACCRA — The Entrepreneur's Handbook
IMPACT GUIDE SERIES STARTUP GUIDE NAIROBI — The Entrepreneur's Handbook
IMPACT GUIDE SERIES STARTUP GUIDE GERMANY — The Entrepreneur's Handbook
IMPACT GUIDE SERIES STARTUP GUIDE KIGALI — The Entrepreneur's Handbook

startupguide.com

Follow us: @StartupGuideHQ

About the Guide

Based on traditional guidebooks and stocked with information you might need to know about starting your next business adventure, Startup Guide books help you navigate and connect with different startup scenes across the globe. Each book is packed with exciting stories of entrepreneurship, insightful interviews with local experts and useful tips and tricks. To date, Startup Guide has featured over fifty cities and regions in Europe, Asia, the US, Africa and the Middle East, including Berlin, London, Singapore, New York, Cape Town and Tel Aviv.

How we make the books:

To ensure an accurate and trustworthy guide every time, we team up with local partners that are established in their respective startup scene. We then ask the local community to nominate startups, coworking spaces, founders, schools, investors, incubators and established businesses to be featured through an online submission form. Based on the results, these submissions are narrowed down to the top one hundred organizations and individuals. Next, the local advisory board – which is selected by our community partners and consists of key players in the local startup community – votes for the final selection, ensuring a balanced representation of industries and startup stories in each book. The local community partners then work in close collaboration with our international editorial and design team to help research, organize interviews with journalists and plan photoshoots. Finally, all content is reviewed and edited and the book is designed and created by the Startup Guide team before going to print in Berlin.

Where to find us:

The easiest way to get your hands on a Startup Guide book is to order it from our online shop: startupguide.com/shop. You can also visit us at our office:

Borgbjergsvej 1
2450 Copenhagen, Denmark
copenhagen@startupguide.com

Want to become a stockist or suggest a store?

Get in touch here: sales@gestalten.com

The Startup Guide Website

Since the first Startup Guide book was published, our network has grown and the possibilities to reach new audiences have expanded. One of the reasons we decided to start producing content through a digital platform was to be able to take a deeper look at the cities, regions and ecosystems that our books cover. We want to make it more accessible for new entrepreneurs to understand the process of getting a startup off the ground through the stories of those who were once in their shoes. By sharing educational content and inspiring examples from the startup community, our website provides valuable insights and continues our core purpose: to guide, empower and inspire people beginning their entrepreneurial path.

For more details, visit our website at startupguide.com.

#startupeverywhere

Startup Guide was founded by Sissel Hansen in 2014. As a publishing and media company, we produce guidebooks and online content to help entrepreneurs navigate and connect with different startup scenes across the globe. As the world of work changes, our mission stays the same: to guide, empower and inspire people to start their own business anywhere. To get your hands on one of our books, feel free to visit us at our office in Copenhagen.

Want to learn more,
become a partner or just say hello? ♥

Send us an email at info@startupguide.com

Follow us: @StartupGuideHQ
Join us and #startupeverywhere

Warsaw Advisory Board

Agata Kwaśniewska
CEO
ReaktorX

Agata Piekut
Communication Manager
Geek Girls Carrots

Artur Kurasiński
CEO
Kurasinski.com

Aureliusz Górski
Cofounder
CIC Innovation Campus

Ewa Geresz
Director of Programs and
Partnerships
Venture Café Warsaw

Grzegorz Marczak
CEO
Antyweb

Karolina Zdrodowska
Head Coordinator
for Entrepreneurship
and Social Dialogue
City of Warsaw

Kinga Lekston
Product Owner
Santander Bank Polska

Konrad Latkowski
Owner
KSYcorp.com

Krzysztof Domaradzki
Journalist
Forbes

Łukasz Skarka
Head of Investments CEE
EIT Innoenergy

Maciej Sadowski
CEO
Startup Hub Poland
Foundation

Marcin Małecki
Editor-in-Chief
MamStartup

Michał Kramarz
Head of Google
for Startups, Central
and Eastern Europe
Google

Paula Pul
Cofounder and
Managing Partner
LAWMORE

WHERE NEXT?

With thanks to our **Content Partners**

Co-funded by the
European Union

Polish Development Fund